DREam
DECODER

DREAM DECODER

Reveal your unconscious desires

DR. FIONA ZUCKER

Quantum
Books

A QUANTUM BOOK

This book is produced by
Quantum Publishing Ltd.
6 Blundell Street
London N7 9BH

Copyright © 2000, 2003 Quarto Publishing plc

This edition printed 2007

All rights reserved.
This book is protected by copyright. No part of it
may be reproduced, stored in a retrieval system, or
transmitted in any form or by any means, without the
prior permission in writing of the Publisher, nor be
otherwise circulated in any form of binding or cover
other than that in which it is published and without a
similar condition including this condition being
imposed on the subsequent publisher.

ISBN 978-1-84573-135-9

QUMDMDC

Printed in China by
SNP Leefung

CONTENTS

MAKING THE MOST OF YOUR DREAMS   **132**

WORLD ⊕F DREAMS

Our dreams can differ from our real lives in many ways. In our dreams we may see and hear things that seem normal—and react to them bizarrely; or we may dream without embarrassment of things that we would consciously find shocking. There is no single explanation of why we dream—or of why we sleep. A multiplicity of physiological and psychological theories of sleep and dreaming have been proposed from the beginning of history to modern times.

NIGHT AND DAY

Sleep is such a regular part of our lives that we rarely consider its nature. When we do stop to think about it, the act of sleeping can seem puzzling. While asleep, we lose consciousness and abandon control of our movements and thoughts. If such an experience were to occur during our waking lives, it would be frightening, yet we endure this process every night. We do know, however, that lack of sleep is detrimental to our health: it causes fatigue, poor concentration, and extreme emotions.

Sleep cycles

Modern sleep analysis began nearly 50 years ago. Interest grew when it was discovered that sleep consists of clearly differentiated phases. These can be determined by the observation of brain waves and general physiological activity. During an average night's sleep, four phases of sleep occur. The cycle of movement from phase one through phase four usually happens about seven times a night. Each cycle lasts approximately 90 minutes.

The four phases

In phase one of the sleep cycle, the sleeper moves from wakefulness to sleep. Phase two marks the beginning of actual sleep, where the sleeper is unaware of outside stimulation. Phase three is a gradual continuation of the transition into deeper sleep. In the final phase, phase four, we sink into an even deeper level of sleep. During this phase, the sleeper breathes more rhythmically and deeply. Heart rate and blood pressure drop, the metabolism slows, and the electrical activity of the brain is different from its waking state. When phase four is complete, the sleeper moves back through the phases, and the physiological changes are reversed: the pulse beats faster and less regularly, the metabolism and electrical activity return to their waking state, the blood pressure increases, the body often moves, and a penile or clitoral erection can occur. As these reverse changes happen, the sleeper seems to be on the verge of waking—yet it is, paradoxically, harder to wake someone at this point than during the deep level of phase four.

REM sleep

Phase four is also known as "rapid eye movement," or REM, sleep. This describes the process whereby the eyes dart rapidly from side to side under closed eyelids— and it marks the onset of dreaming. Dreams can happen in phases one, two, or three of the sleep cycle, but they are less frequent and not as vivid as those occurring in REM sleep. It is hypothesized that the rapid movements of the eye may actually represent the dreamer's observation of the events that are taking place in the dream.

In 1953, the American physiologist Nathaniel Kleitman and his student Eugene Aserinsky pioneered a clinical study of dreaming. They discovered that if a sleeper was awakened during the time when the electrical impulses of the brain exhibited certain rhythms, he or she reported dreaming at that time. The periods of brain activity and dreaming also corresponded with the occurrence of rapid eye movements. These discoveries marked the beginning of an intense period of study of dreaming and dream patterns.

Why do we sleep?

Aristotle believed that during sleep the body emitted certain vapors, which helped disperse food from the stomach to the rest of the body. In a similar vein, some researchers in the early 20th century maintained that chemicals such as carbon dioxide, cholesterol and lactic acid collect in the brain during waking hours, and sleep provides an opportunity for these chemicals to be redistributed throughout the body.

Another popular theory postulated that sleep was merely a means of regaining energy. It seemed unlikely, however, that this explanation was complete, as it failed to account for the evident need for REM sleep in particular. Newborn babies, for example, spend about half of their sleeping time in the REM state; evidence of an REM state has also been observed in most mammals, birds, and reptiles. Further, experiments have shown that people deprived of REM sleep become excessively sensitive, lose the ability to concentrate, and suffer poor recall. In contrast, those deprived of non-REM sleep experience fewer and shorter-term difficulties. It thus appears that in non-REM sleep, the body and mind are resting and regenerating. REM sleep, on the other hand, seems to be less physiologically but more psychologically important.

The nature of dreams

Despite the large body of research into sleeping patterns, the human need to dream continues to evoke more questions than answers. Are dreams a way to dispel unwanted waking experiences? Are they a means of processing daily events? Or are they an exercise for a part of the brain that remains dormant during the waking hours?

As a result of studying dreams in laboratories, which allows for "on the spot" dream retrieval, scientists have discovered that the vast majority of dreams, including those experienced during an REM state, are mundane, highly realistic experiences, as opposed to bizarre, random occurrences. Further, dreams are also not usually faithful reproductions of memories; rather, they are novel experiences which have a thematic coherence, much like a story or novel. In most dreams, the dreamer experiences emotions that are appropriate to the particular situation in the dream.

It seems likely that dreaming has a number of complex and interrelated physiological and psychological functions. One thing is clear, however: the dreams of each individual encapsulate aspects of his or her particular psyche and circumstances, including his or her life situation, relationships, and experiences. An awareness of our dreams, therefore, may help us to increase our understanding of our thoughts and emotions.

ANCIENT DREAMERS

Human beings have long been fascinated by dreams and their meanings. The earliest dream interpreters believed that dreams were a means of communication with the gods. During the 12th dynasty (c. 1991–1786 BC), Egyptian thinkers began to record the symbols that appeared in people's dreams, and to ponder their meanings. The Babylonians and the ancient Hebrews were also fascinated by the world of dreams, and took some of their inspiration from the Egyptian writings. The ancient Hebrews took dream analysis a step further and considered the influence of the dreamer's waking life as well, including the person's family life, personal qualities, and occupation.

Dream messages

In the 8th century BC, Homer's epic poem, "The Iliad," referred to a dream message. Zeus, the King of the gods, sent a message in a dream to Agamemnon, the commander of the Greek forces at Troy. Like the Egyptians, the Greeks believed that dreams held curative powers. People in need of healing would sleep in temples for long periods of time in the hope of experiencing a dream that would forecast recovery.

In the 5th century BC, ideas about dreams began changing, and the role of the supernatural in dream interpretation became less prominent. Some Greek philosophers proposed that dreams were products of the individual, and were unconnected to others—even to the world of the gods. Plato (c. 428–348 BC) was especially interested in the influence of dreams on a person's mental and physical life, and believed that dreamed messages could signal how a person should lead his or her life. In his famous dialogue *Phaedo*, he noted that Socrates's decision to follow music and the arts was the result of a dream.

> *"Up, go, thou baneful Dream, unto the swift ships of the Achaeans, and when thou art come to the hut of Agamemnon, son of Atreus, tell him all my word truly, even as I charge thee."*
>
> **The Iliad**

In ancient Egypt, people who were emotionally troubled would sometimes have their dreams analyzed by a priest—an interesting precursor to Freudian psychoanalysis.

Metaphors and medicine

For Aristotle (384–322 BC), dreams were usually not prophetic; rather, they related to memories of the dreamer's waking day. Aristotle also wrote of dreams being "ignited" by the human senses. If a person became very hot when sleeping, for example, he or she might dream about heat or fire.

Aristotle thought that metaphor was crucial in dream analysis. He suggested that dream images were not simply reflections of the waking world, but metaphors for other images and situations. This view forms the basis of modern dream analysis.

Before Aristotle, the physician Hippocrates (c. 460–357 BC)—the founder of modern medicine—believed in dreams as a diagnostic tool. Other Greek thinkers also subscribed to this theory; as a result, many ancient Greeks were medically treated based on dreams that featured ailing parts of their bodies.

Roman interpretations

Around 150 AD, the Roman scholar Artemidorus compiled a five-volume work entitled *Oneirocriticon* ("The Interpretation of Dreams"). In this work, he espoused the theory that dreams

were rooted in the dreamer's waking world. When a dream was interpreted, therefore, the dreamer's social status, place of work, and mental and physical condition should all be considered when attempting to decipher its content and meaning.

Old Testament dreams

Many dreams and dream symbols feature in the Old Testament. In one well-known story, Jacob's favorite son Joseph was said to possess the power of predictive dreams. Since they often contained images of Joseph's superiority to his brothers, the dreams were responsible for a serious bout of sibling rivalry. Joseph's brothers contrived to exile him, while convincing their father that Joseph was dead. Joseph's skills at dream analysis proved useful, however, when he was able to help the mighty Pharaoh of Egypt interpret a troubling dream.

Daniel was another famous dream interpreter, and was asked to interpret a dream for the King of Babylon, Nebuchadnezzar. In the dream, a message from Heaven ordered that a beautiful tree, which sheltered all the animals of the universe, should be cut down, and that Nebuchadnezzar should be chained to the remains of the tree. Daniel interpreted the dream as a message to the King that despite his position of majesty, he must accept a greater power in heaven as the ultimate ruler.

New Testament visions

Some of the most striking illustrations of the New Testament portray biblical dream visions. In an interpretation of the New Testament written in the 4th century AD, St. John Chrysostom stated that God revealed Himself and His message through dreams. St. John also believed that people were not responsible for the content of their dreams, and thus should not feel guilty about any shameful images appearing therein.

Perhaps the best known dream in the Old Testament is Jacob's dream of a ladder resting on top of the Earth reaching up to the heavens—the means of communication between God's angels and the Earth.

Religious revelations

Dreams are significant in Islam as well. The prophet Mohammed, the founder of Islam, is said to have become aware of much of the Koran's contents from a dream. He was also well known for interpreting the dreams of his disciples.

Originating from India is a long Buddhist tradition of dream interpretation. The Buddha's mother had a dream in which a tiny white elephant entered her womb. Brahmins claimed that this dream predicted the birth of a great ruler.

For Zoroastrians, dreams are linked to their time of occurrence, so that a dream's place within the monthly cycle will affect its interpretation.

WORLD DREAMERS

There is a long history of dream analysis in Western tradition, but dream interpretation within other cultures is equally rich—and often markedly different. For Native Americans, dreams and their messages are ways of predicting and understanding events. In many Eastern traditions, it is widely accepted that the dreamer can actually influence his or her dream world.

Eastern dream analysis

Many Eastern dream analysts believe that a dreamer can actually take control of his or her dream world and thereby pursue a path of personal growth and spiritual development. Some even claim—in contrast to most Western thinkers—that the dreamer can remain conscious while dreaming. Moreover, it is this conscious dreaming that enables the dreamer to gain the greatest spiritual rewards.

Some Eastern philosophers describe the process of sleeping as a preparation for death. Each time we sleep, we ready ourselves for the time when we must die. It is thus in the dreamer's interest to prepare for sleeping and dreaming in the calmest and most comfortable way possible.

Native American dreams

Different Native American tribes use a variety of techniques to induce the dream state and to interpret dreams, but all share a profound belief in the willpower of the dreamer. According to this belief, the dreamer can will the occurrence of a specific type of dream by concentrating upon the desired themes in the pre-dream state. The dream that follows can act as a guide to show the dreamer how he or she should act upon waking. Preparations for the desired dream include praying, meditating, and fasting. Spending time at a peaceful and secluded location is also seen as an important inducement for entering the dream state.

Native Americans believe that they can encounter a spiritual guide in their dreams, who may then assist them in some capacity. This spirit helper, who can reappear repeatedly in dreams, may impart a specific piece of knowledge or skill within the dream, such as a way of understanding an object, or an aspect of the animal kingdom.

Dream control

In the Malaysian jungle, the Senoi people have developed their own form of dream interpretation. They believe that dreams can be controlled and modified in a positive sense while they are occurring. Thus a dreamer

facing danger should tackle it head on. If something good happens in the dream, the dreamer should approach and embrace it; if evil is told to the dreamer, he or she should refuse to listen. In this way, Senoi interpretations are connected to the dreamer's emotional development. Learning to deal with dream fears, for example, can help the dreamer to manage real fears; welcoming pleasure in dreams can engender positive attitudes during wakefulness.

Dreaming is therefore a two-way process: just as our waking emotions affect our dreams, the reverse can also occur.

A shared experience

In the Australian Aboriginal tradition, the recounting of dreams is a frequent, shared experience. For some tribes, if a dream subverts the expectations of the community—such as a man's sexual dream about a woman who is not his wife—something in the dream is expected to intercede.

Dreams play a crucial role in Aboriginal tradition, which holds that the universe was created from a series of dreams.

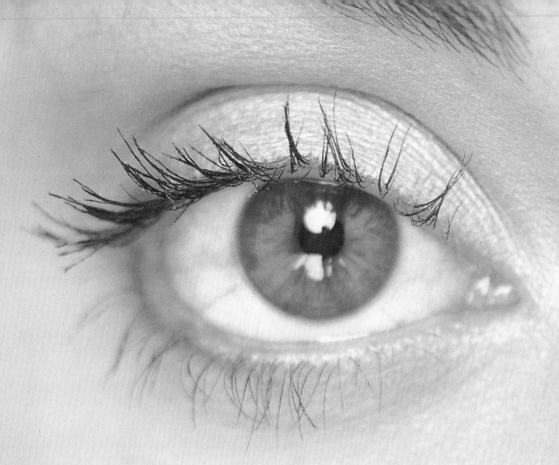

THE PSYCHOLOGY OF DREAMS

Any study of modern dream analysis should begin with the theories of its founding fathers: the Austrian psychiatrist Sigmund Freud (1856-1939) and his Swiss associate, Carl Gustav Jung (1875-1961). These theories are widely held to be the basis of all contemporary dream analysis.

Conscious v. unconscious

The conscious mind—which operates while we are awake—is defined as comprising the thoughts and images that go through a person's mind during wakefulness, and of which he or she is fully aware. The unconscious mind refers to repressed thoughts, feelings, and memories of which the person is not fully aware. Psychologists believe that the unconscious influences emotions and behavior, but it cannot be accessed at will. Hypnosis, free association, and meditation may help to reach the unconscious, but the main means of access is through dreams.

Freud's interpretation

Sigmund Freud pioneered the use of dreams as a way of connecting with a person's unconscious mind. His classic text *The Interpretation of Dreams* (1899) essentially summarized the study of dreams over the centuries, and was extremely influential for two reasons: it established the concept that dreams and dreaming merited serious scientific study, and it addressed which questions to ask in relation to dream analysis.

Freud examined what the purpose of dreaming might be. He also considered how dreams might serve as vehicles for learning more about the workings of the human mind. He believed that the successful interpretation of dreams could have significant implications for the treatment of psychological problems, and that dreams could be used to monitor a patient's progress.

Deep desires

Freud argued that the mind operates on both a primary and a secondary level. During the act of dreaming, a "primary process" occurs, in which the dreamer's unconscious desires or fears are turned into symbols, which then appear in the dream. The "secondary process" refers to the repression of these impulses and

symbols by the conscious waking mind.

For Freud, dreams were generally intertwined with the dreamer's deepest desires. Further, much of the basis of dreams, he asserted, derived from emotions or experiences that took place in childhood. Freud also claimed that dreams were often the mind's way of expressing sexual or erotic desires, and that many dream images were symbols of sexuality. Thus, in his interpretations, long objects were often related to the penis, and certain fruits were associated with breasts.

The id and the ego

Freud identified the id as the part of the mind that contains our primitive instincts, and the ego as the part of the mind concerned with morality, logic, and rationality. When we dream, he contended, the id enacts our unconscious desires.

The function of dream symbols, according to Freud, was to allow humans to continue sleeping while permitting the id to express animalistic desires. Thus the desires are enacted, but do not enter the conscious mind unless the dream symbols are interpreted.

Freud based many of his dream interpretations on the concept of the id and the repressed desires of the unconscious mind. By the 1920s, many scientists and psychologists disagreed with his theory. In their view, dreams did not unlock our hidden desires; rather, they were extensions and reflections of the dreamer's waking life. Freud eventually revised his ideas, making a distinction between dreams inspired by the id and dreams that were rooted in the experiences of a person's waking life.

Free association

Freud developed the idea of free association, an exercise thought to enable the dreamer to access his or her unconscious mind during waking life. Broadly speaking, the technique involves three stages. In the first stage, the dreamer focuses on a recent dream. In the second stage, the dreamer allows his or her mind to drift, and sees what words or images come to mind in association with the dream. In the third stage, the dreamer and the analyst try to establish if the "associated" words or images have any meaning for the dreamer, and whether they prompt the recall of a forgotten memory or the surge of a particular emotion.

Jung's interpretation

Carl Jung collaborated with Freud for a time, but they eventually parted ways due to academic differences. Jung agreed with Freud that dreams generally represent the dreamer's unconscious mind, but questioned whether dreams were solely the product of the the dreamer's personal experiences.

Jung began to look for identical themes in the dreams of different individuals. He discovered notable similarities between the dream imagery, associations, and delusions of a broad range of his psychotic patients. Jung also had a keen interest in mythology, world religions, and the occult, and he noticed associations between key elements of those studies and recurrent themes in people's dreams. He believed that these common themes derived from a shared body of historical and cultural myths and stories throughout the world. Jung concluded that there must exist some form of "collective unconscious," an inborn store of information, linked with a human tendency to organize and interpret experiences in similar ways regardless of culture and background. In this way, Jung introduced the concept of a universal "archetype"—an innate idea or pattern that could emerge within dreams in the form of a basic symbol or image. Dreams, he argued, contained a range of such archetypes. Jung referred to dreams involving archetypes as "grand dreams."

Archetypes
Jung described archetypes as primeval images and ideas that contain meaning for all people at all times. He claimed that archetypes were not only expressed in dreams, but in forms of folklore such as fairy tales and legends as well.

The archetypes are personalized according to each individual's experience, but readily recognizable examples include the wicked witch, the wise old man, the beautiful woman, the cheat, the hero, and the magician. According to Jung, dream symbols can only be properly understood when related to their archetypal meanings. In Jungian interpretation, therefore, it is essential to have knowledge of the range of archetypes, and to consider what each archetype might represent to the dreamer.

Jung v. Freud
Jung was convinced that Freud's method of free association led the dreamer away from the dream, and could cause the dreamer to lose touch with the important symbols contained therein. He therefore developed a technique which he termed "direct association," which required dreamers to reflect on and make associations with specific aspects of the dream rather than dwelling on the dream as a whole.

Jung's dreamwork
In his quest to unravel the meanings of dreams, Jung analyzed every dream occurrence in three distinct contexts: the personal, the cultural, and the archetypal.

Jung believed that dreams exercised an almost religious function, because they helped to guide people on journeys of self-discovery. He contended that dreams could contribute to a process that points individuals in the direction of spiritual enlightenment. For Jung, therefore, the dream was not just a reflection of repressed desires or a form of wish fulfillment, but also a conduit through which people could make a connection with their "higher" or wiser selves. The dream could also reveal the roots of a person's present problems, and might contain clues about how to solve them.

Spiritual growth
Jung chose the basement of a beautiful house as his image of the place that most humans inhabit. The house, with its fascinating and diverse rooms, represents the enormous potential for creative and spiritual growth possessed by all human beings. Many of us, however, confine ourselves to the basement, and do not realize our potential by

exploring the rest of the house. For Jung, dreams were a means of gaining access to the other rooms of the house, and dream interpretation was the means of exploration.

Coded messages

Like Freud, Jung thought dreams were highly symbolic, and stressed that they should not be taken at face value. Dreams impart coded messages, he contended, but these are only released in segments that our conscious minds can understand and assimilate. Jung believed that the more people understood about dreams and their various layers of meaning, the more they would understand various aspects of their personal and emotional lives.

Perls and the personal

The founder of Gestalt therapy, Fritz Perls (1893-1970) believed that all dream symbols were projections of the dreamer's own world, and of the way in which the dreamer wished to lead his or her life. Moreover, the symbols expressed elements of the dreamer's psychology unacknowledged by the dreamer in waking life. He thus rejected Jung's idea of dream symbols as part of some universal language, seeing them as the highly personalized creations of each dreamer. He also rejected Freud's notion that held that dreams represent instinctive or repressed desires, instead believing them to reflect the dreamer's waking experiences.

For Perls, the dream reflected unresolved personal and emotional issues not yet dealt with in waking life. The therapeutic value of dreams consisted in establishing the exact personal meanings behind the dream images; this would help the dreamer solve his or her emotional difficulties. To help interpret dream imagery, Perls developed a series of role-play exercises, in which the dreamer took the part of each character or object which featured in the dream.

Perls's approach to dream analysis differed markedly from those of Freud and Jung, in that his dreamers were asked to conduct their own interpretation instead of relying on that of the dream analyst. He thought it necessary that a dreamer interpret his or her own dreams, using his or her own life experience. The therapist, or members of a therapeutic group, could contribute suggestions, but the dreamer must discover the dream's significance him- or herself, without the imposition of any outside meaning.

Meaningless dreams

Medard Boss was one of the principal founders of existential psychology, a theory which holds that each person chooses his or her life's direction, and expresses that choice through all aspects of his or her behavior. In 1958, Boss wrote *The Analysis of Dreams*, in which he maintained that the events in a dream should not be broken down into symbols; rather, they should be taken at face value. Dreams are simply a representation of life, he asserted, and because life is meaningless, dreams also have no meaning.

Some psychologists agree with Boss's non-symbolic approach to dream study, but see dreams as having a function. In this view, dreams are a means of disposing of memories that would otherwise clutter our minds with too many emotions and experiences.

DIRECTORY OF DREAM SYMBOLS

Although dreaming is by nature a personal experience, it is clear that there are certain themes that appear consistently in most people's dreams. These themes can be identified by the images, or symbols, that occur within them. Thus, careful consideration of the meaning of each symbol in a dream will help uncover its overriding theme, and, ultimately, its meaning. The feelings experienced by the dreamer in the dream can also provide clues to its meaning.

DREAM FINDER

Below is a guide to the dream symbols interpreted within this book. It can also be used as a quick-reference tool to discover the positive messages, negative implications, and emotions commonly associated with each dream symbol.

LIFE AND DEATH

	POSITIVE	NEGATIVE	EMOTIONS
Baby SEE PAGE 29	An original idea may soon demand your attention	A hungry baby implies a desire for physical or spiritual nourishment	You may be seeking to contact your inner child
Birthday SEE PAGE 30	Birthday dreams often portend good luck	A forgotten birthday implies a fear of loneliness	Fears of aging and the rapid passing of time may be reflected
Wedding SEE PAGE 31	Dreaming of your own wedding implies a new relationship will last	Perhaps you shouldn't try so hard in your quest for the perfect mate	Happy feelings at your dream wedding imply confidence that a relationship will last
Drowning SEE PAGE 32	Dreams of drowning imply the overcoming of obstacles	A drowning dream may indicate that you feel out of control	A sensation of feeling overwhelmed by your current situation is implied
Pregnancy SEE PAGE 32	Can be a form of wish fulfillment	If you don't want to have a baby, you may fear the prospect of giving birth	The nurturing side of your personality is being reflected
Baptism SEE PAGE 33	A new project or initiative will prove successful	Future unforeseen circumstances may bring disappointment	A desire to become stronger and more assertive is implied
Buried alive SEE PAGE 33	You have laid a particular matter to rest	Ill fortune and difficult times may lie ahead	You may be feeling trapped in a particular situation
Funeral SEE PAGE 33	A funeral dream can foretell future celebration	Enduring hostility toward the deceased may be reflected	Sadness in the dream may mean you should examine your feelings toward the deceased
Skeleton SEE PAGE 33	Demonstration skeletons can predict the arrival of new colleagues	You may be concerned about a domestic problem	A fear of humiliation is implied
Killing SEE PAGE 34	Positive change—the end of the old and the beginning of the new—is implied	You may be feeling intense emotional stress	Someone or something may have aroused bitterness, envy, or anger within you

FORCES OF NATURE

	POSITIVE	NEGATIVE	EMOTIONS
Earthquake SEE PAGE **39**	Earth tremors may presage the arrival of positive change	To see your loved ones in an earthquake dream suggests that they may need your help	If you were frightened, the dream may reflect a worry in your daily life
Volcano SEE PAGE **39**	Volcano dreams can represent a shift in your internal world	A dormant volcano may warn about the reliability of new projects	Consider the strength of the eruption and your reaction to it
Fire SEE PAGE **40**	A fire in a hearth at home can indicate comfort	Something in your waking life may need purging	The fire can symbolize light, spirituality, or inner power
Ocean SEE PAGE **42**	A calm ocean can foretell untroubled times	Engulfment by waves may denote a fear of your repressed emotions	A dream ocean can represent your emotional life
Ice SEE PAGE **43**	Ice dreams outside winter can signify a fruitful harvest, or the fruition of ideas	It may be time to get a project you had put on ice underway	Bitter cold usually represents an emotional extreme
Sky SEE PAGE **44**	A clear sky can announce pleasurable times ahead	A cloudy sky may forecast turbulent times ahead	The vastness of a dream sky can represent creative potential
Sun SEE PAGE **44**	To dream of a sunrise can foretell positive news	A setting sun suggests a downward spiral in your life	A bright sun can signify interior strength
Hail SEE PAGE **45**	The end of a hailstorm can foretell a positive life change	Being caught in a hailstorm may signify jealousy	Enjoyment of the icy stones on your face can indicate that you like rising to challenges
Lightning SEE PAGE **45**	A sudden flash of lightning can indicate a bright idea	If the lightning damaged anything, consider what that article represents for you	Lightning dreams are usually related to inspiration and power
Star SEE PAGE **45**	A starry sky can signal prosperous times	Pale stars can signify future difficulties	Nearness to the dream star can reflect proximity to achieving your ambitions
Storm SEE PAGE **45**	If you found shelter, you may find a resolution to a romantic problem	Storm dreams can be connected to worries about obstacles	The duration of the storm can reflect the magnitude of your problems
River SEE PAGE **46**	Crossing a river implies a significant life change	Falling in a river can warn of future domestic concerns	Did the dream river frighten you—or calm you?
Thunder SEE PAGE **46**	Thunder close by can signify victory or marital happiness	A thunderbolt nearby suggests you need a change in your life	Booming thunder indicates that a problem will soon be solved
Moon SEE PAGE **47**	A bright moon may foretell personal or career changes	A moon shadowed by the sun can be a negative omen	Flying to the moon implies a desire to travel
Planets SEE PAGE **47**	A significant life change may be ahead	Dreaming of other planets implies dissatisfaction with your daily routine	You may be feeling the need to make a radical life change

VEGETATION AND NATURAL SURROUNDINGS

	POSITIVE	NEGATIVE	EMOTIONS
Flowers SEE PAGE 51	Everyday flowers can be linked to feelings of security	A wreath is often associated with feelings of hostility	Sending flowers implies a need for recognition
Grass SEE PAGE 52	A well-kept lawn can symbolize a well-organized work project	Overgrown grass implies stress in your waking life	How large was the expanse of grass? What color was it?
Trees SEE PAGE 52	A healthy tree can reflect the potential to achieve goals	A decaying or dead tree can symbolize displeasure or fear	Dream trees can symbolize your perception of the status of your personal growth
Branches SEE PAGE 53	Branches swaying in the wind suggest new activities ahead	Broken branches imply concern about problems	The branches may represent your familial relationships; note how and if they were growing
Bush SEE PAGE 53	Healthy bushes are usually linked to notions of support	A bush without foliage can warn not to rely on luck	Pruning a bush can mean a secret will soon be revealed
Hill/mountain SEE PAGE 53	Standing on top of a hill or mountain is a sign of pride and honor	Struggling up a hill or mountain suggests a problem may be hard to overcome	Any help you received in your climb can be a reflection of how supported you feel in life
Leaves SEE PAGE 53	A fruit tree's leaves can foretell good financial luck	Wind swept leaves can signify a family argument	The position of the leaves on the tree may reflect how contained you feel in your life
Fruit SEE PAGE 54	Gathering fruit in season can signify personal happiness	Rotting fruit may be connected to the premature end of a chapter in your life	Dream fruit may symbolize the unconscious development of your inner self

PEOPLE AND PLACES

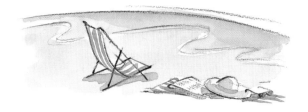

	POSITIVE	NEGATIVE	EMOTIONS
Bride & bridegroom SEE PAGE 59	Wish fulfillment is implied, especially if you were the bride or groom	You may be feeling jealousy or rivalry	A commitment to a current relationship—or a fear of commitment—is implied
Father & mother SEE PAGE 60	Dreaming of your parents can express your love for them in waking life	A dream in which your parents die implies feelings of hostility toward them	The way you view your parents in a dream can represent how you view them in waking life
Castle SEE PAGE 62	A beautiful dream castle can foretell a comfortable future	A dream castle in disrepair warns of financial hardship	The dream castle may be a representation of yourself
Place of worship SEE PAGE 62	Participation in a religious ritual can signify joy	Shunning a religious building or service implies that you are feeling guilty	Moral issues are at the forefront of your mind; you may also be seeking higher guidance
Beach SEE PAGE 63	A desire for liberation or escape is implied	You may be keeping a secret from someone close to you	How did you feel while on the dream beach?
Desert island SEE PAGE 63	Romance may be headed your way	Being cast upon a desert island can symbolize rejection	You may be yearning to escape crowds—or for an end to loneliness
Familiar places SEE PAGE 63	Satisfaction with your past and contentment with your present is implied	Dissatisfaction with your current situation is implied	Your reaction to the familiar place can reflect whether you have learned from your past
Fence SEE PAGE 63	Climbing a fence can signify overcoming an obstacle	A high fence blocking your way suggests restriction	A dream fence can represent feelings of being challenged
Park SEE PAGE 64	Park dreams can symbolize a sense of fulfillment	You may need to discover some personal space	The dream park may reflect the way you have organized your life
Workplace SEE PAGE 64	A positive change in your love life may arise	Ejection from your office implies a loss of property or personal possessions	Your feelings while in the dream office can have implications for your work or home life
Cellar SEE PAGE 65	A journey or an expansion of work or business interests is implied	You may feel trapped or out of touch	A dream cellar can represent the deepest levels of your mind
Stairways SEE PAGE 65	Stairways can portray success and progress	An endless stairway can signify struggle	Ascending or descending a stairway may represent aspects of your sexual self
House SEE PAGE 66	Building a house can denote fortuitous business opportunities	If your house was destroyed, you may need to make changes in your daily life	House dreams often reflect your emotional and spiritual state
Kings & Queens SEE PAGE 68	Dream kings symbolize honor and respect; dream queens represent intuition	You may need to face up to certain responsibilities	Dreams involving royalty often focus on passivity, or the sensation of being a subject

HUMAN BODY

	POSITIVE	NEGATIVE	EMOTIONS
Breasts SEE PAGE **73**	Dream breasts are often connected with nature and growth	Dreaming about breasts can imply excessive attachment to a mother figure	Breasts can symbolize Mother Earth
Buttocks SEE PAGE **73**	Kicking someone in the buttocks can imply a desire for a promotion	Aiming to kick someone's buttocks but missing can signify a project may fail	If the dream was sexual, it may be linked to your sexual desires
Blood SEE PAGE **74**	A blood transfusion implies you are on the verge of solving a problem	A loss of blood can represent deterioration	An easy flow of blood can signify the feeling that you are on the right path in life
Ears SEE PAGE **75**	Many ears can mean you feel respected by work colleagues	Possession of a wild animal's ears may imply fears of deception	Ear dreams can be about listening to others—or to your unconscious
Hair SEE PAGE **76**	An unfamiliar woman with beautiful hair can predict friendship and happiness	Tangled or braided hair may indicate complex problems	Well-groomed hair implies a healthy inner self
Teeth SEE PAGE **76**	Gleaming teeth can symbolize wealth or friendship	One tooth larger than the rest implies anxiety about a disappointment	Dreams involving the roots of teeth can refer to the stability of your relationships
Feet SEE PAGE **77**	Bathing your feet suggests distance from your worries	Many feet walking together may signify material loss	The strength or determination of the feet can indicate how you are approaching a task
Hands SEE PAGE **77**	Caressed hands suggest friendship or romance	Dirty hands can be a warning to curb bad behavior	The dexterity of dream hands can relate to personal matters
Legs SEE PAGE **77**	Healthy, strong legs imply contentment	A wooden leg suggests over-reliance on external help	Itchy legs may be a sign to stop worrying
Spine SEE PAGE **77**	A straight spine can signify inner strength and determination	A curved spine may reveal a lack of will	The straightness of the spine can reflect feelings of unity with your unconscious
Eyes SEE PAGE **78**	Dreams involving sharp sight can be positive omens	Troubled sight implies a need for financial assistance	You may need to pay attention to a message from your unconscious
Face SEE PAGE **80**	A beautiful dream face with no resemblance to your own can indicate pride	An unknown dream face can symbolize life changes	Cleansing your face in a dream may reflect feelings of guilt

animals

	POSITIVE	NEGATIVE	EMOTIONS
Bull SEE PAGE 85	A dream bull may represent a special figure in your life	An attacking bull can mean someone is talking about you behind your back	Your ability to harness the bull implies successful integration of your animalistic nature
Fox SEE PAGE 85	Capturing or killing a fox implies you will outwit those who plot against you	Danger may lie ahead—be on your guard	You may need to be more open in your dealings with others—or more wily
Cat SEE PAGE 86	Cats are associated with fertility and new beginnings	A dead or chased cat foretells bad luck; a scratching cat implies territorial defense	An angry, cussing cat can symbolize a catty aspect of your personality
Horse SEE PAGE 87	You are at ease with yourself and your surroundings	Fearing a dream horse implies anxiety about losing an object	The horse's pace can reflect how you view the pace of your life
Bird SEE PAGE 88	Good fortune and unlimited possibilities may lie ahead	You may be seeking escape from a particular situation	Feelings of independence and personal strength are implied
Dolphin SEE PAGE 90	You are successfully meeting cerebral challenges	You may need to move on to new challenges	Your unconscious self may be trying to communicate with your conscious self
Fish SEE PAGE 90	A dream of many fish may predict good fortune	Fish in a dream implies greed or lust over material possessions	Many fish in a dream can represent an encounter with your true self
Mouse SEE PAGE 91	You may receive some good or promising news shortly	Strife or discord may be present among your family or friends	You may be seeking greater emotional strength
Rabbit SEE PAGE 91	Eating a dream rabbit can mean you enjoy your work and are successful at it	A dream of many rabbits implies fears of being undermined by enemies	New responsibilities that you will happily take on may lie ahead
Snake SEE PAGE 91	Attacking a snake implies overcoming those who wish to see you fail	A coiled snake indicates danger or restriction	Snake dreams can highlight your innate wisdom or sexuality
Tiger SEE PAGE 91	Escaping from a tiger is generally a good omen	Being caught by a tiger can foretell potential danger	A tiger can represent the manipulative components of your personality
Lion SEE PAGE 92	Lions in dreams can relate to your leadership skills	You may be worrying about criticism from an authority figure	Riding on the back of a lion implies that you need support
Dog SEE PAGE 94	Dog dreams may relate to friendship, commitment, loyalty, and devotion	An aggressive dog can signify fear of attack	Your dream dog may represent someone you know
Wolf SEE PAGE 95	Defeating a wolf in a fight can signify overcoming difficult obstacles	If a dream wolf bit you, you may fear harm from adversaries	You may fear the animal within you, or feel sexually repressed

ACTIONS AND SITUATIONS

	POSITIVE	NEGATIVE	EMOTIONS
Gardening SEE PAGE 99	Future gain and financial success may lie ahead	Sadness may be present in your life	The garden's condition can reflect the state of your psyche
Shopping SEE PAGE 99	Shopping dreams can relate to notions of freedom and choice	Hurried shopping can show a lack of self-restraint	Your current emotional needs may be reflected
Chasing or being chased SEE PAGE 100	You are working hard and expect to be rewarded	Being chased can imply a missed deadline or a threat	Dreams of chases can represent uncertainty or anxiety
Nakedness SEE PAGE 101	Nakedness may foretell good luck or financial fortune	You may be longing for childhood innocence	You may be seeking to get beyond superficiality in your relationships
Exams SEE PAGE 102	Dreams of passing an exam may predict positive achievements	Failing an exam may imply an inability to achieve ambitions	Such dreams can be linked to feeling unprepared
Surgery SEE PAGE 102	Dream operations can foretell good fortune or news	An obstacle may need to be overcome	You may be considering changes or improvements in your life
Sex SEE PAGE 103	Sexual dreams can reflect sexual desires or past sexual encounters	You may feel repressed or stifled in your sex life	The integration of connecting energies is implied
Washing/bathing SEE PAGE 103	Washing in clear water can signify personal happiness	Bathing with clothes on can indicate imminent threat	You may be seeking to purify your life
Climbing SEE PAGE 104	Climbing dreams can symbolize current prosperity	Never reaching your destination implies fear of failure	Your feelings during the climb can express your feelings about your progress in life

EVERYDAY ITEMS

	POSITIVE	NEGATIVE	EMOTIONS
Tools SEE PAGE 109	A dream involving leverage implies a wish for increased personal growth	A plow can signify that steady work is needed to tackle emotional problems	Some tools have sexual connotations
Money SEE PAGE 110	Receiving money in a dream is seen as a positive sign	Changing paper money for coins can denote problems in your financial strategy	Spending freely can indicate feelings of goodwill
Jewelry SEE PAGE 111	Receiving jewelry as a present denotes you feel recognized	Viewing a rare jewel you don't own can foretell failure to value a future friendship	Lost jewelry may reflect fears of loss in your waking life
Broom SEE PAGE 112	New brooms traditionally foretell good luck	A damaged broom can reveal feelings of insecurity	Think about any waking life associations with the area that was being swept out

		NEGATIVE	EMOTIONS
Garbage SEE PAGE 112	You may wish to rid your life of wasteful elements	Others disposing of your garbage implies concern that others carry your burdens	Consider how you felt after the garbage was disposed of
Envelope SEE PAGE 113	Open envelopes can predict the onset of trivial problems	Sealed envelopes can signal difficult obstacles ahead	Inability to open an envelope can symbolize frustration
Scissors SEE PAGE 113	An unused pair of scissors can predict future romance	You may be dividing your time between two projects	The scissors may represent an extension of your personality
Food & Drink SEE PAGE 114	Pleasurable consumption of food and drink implies satisfaction with your life	Eating and drinking ravenously suggests unfulfilled needs	The quality and quantity of the food can represent the degree to which you feel fulfilled in life
Cutlery SEE PAGE 116	A spoon can symbolize enduring domestic happiness	A knife implies that a pleasure is about to be cut off	Having difficulty using your cutlery may signify frustration
Containers SEE PAGE 117	A neatly packed container can signify the overcoming of obstacles	A container packed with personal effects implies the need for spring cleaning	A leaky container can suggest the need for caution

TRAVEL

	POSITIVE	NEGATIVE	EMOTIONS
Boat SEE PAGE 121	A boat in a dream can portray a future journey	Rough seas may indicate a period of emotional turmoil	The vessel can symbolize your home life or present emotional well-being
Luggage SEE PAGE 122	Carrying luggage may forecast a long trip	Lost luggage can reflect anxiety	Luggage may symbolize elements in your life that should be disposed of
Highways & roads SEE PAGE 124	Straight roads signify smooth progress in your life	Twisting roads suggest difficulties in the near future	Dream roads can represent the direction your life is taking
Missed transportation SEE PAGE 125	You may be trying to avoid a visit to an undesirable place	Missing your ride can reflect uncertainty about fulfilling your potential	Missed transportation suggests a fear of missing an opportunity at work
Bus SEE PAGE 126	Traveling by bus implies that you are on your way to achieving your goals	Prolonged waiting at a bus stop symbolizes frustration	Was the ride smooth or bumpy?
Passenger SEE PAGE 126	You may be passing your responsibilities off to someone else	Being a passenger can mean you feel out of control	A group of passengers can represent aspects of your emotional self
Airplane SEE PAGE 127	Piloting an airplane can represent an unexpected success	Airplanes dropping bombs can foretell bad news	Feelings of freedom and release are implied
Train SEE PAGE 127	You feel a sense of security about your direction in life	A stationary train can mean a hitch in your plans	A train is thought to represent the male sexual organ
Automobile SEE PAGE 128	You have the chance to make a comfortable living	A car wreck can indicate conflict and a lack of control	A car in your dream may be related to your personal drive

LIFE and DEATH

*D*reams involving the key stages of life often indicate beginnings or endings in areas of the dreamer's waking world. Dreams about joyful life events can represent opportunities for renewal and growth, while dreams about death tend to reflect unconscious anger or frustration, and may represent a wish to move on.

POSITIVE MESSAGES

Baby dreams often suggest creativity and hope. They can symbolize an idea or project that will soon demand your attention—your "brainchild." Baby dreams also imply an attempt to connect with the creative part of your personality.

NEGATIVE IMPLICATIONS

If the baby seems hungry, dissatisfied, or deprived, part of you may be in need of physical or spiritual nourishment.

EMOTIONS

The baby in the dream may be a reflection of you. The dream may symbolize a desire to make contact with your "inner child," or a yearning to return to your childhood. If the baby in the dream appears sick, this can indicate a concern in your working or personal life.

BABY

Many expectant mothers, or those planning to conceive, have vivid dreams about pregnancy, childbirth, and newborn infants. These dreams may simply echo the events of waking life, but sometimes symbolic interpretations need to be considered.

Dreams about babies or giving birth frequently illustrate ideas of growth, nurturing, and new beginnings. The dreamer should listen to his or her dream baby and assess whether he or she represents the dreamer or someone else. If the infant represents the dreamer, this may signify his or her own vulnerability and desire to be cared for. The baby in the dream can also symbolize the dreamer's original, innocent self, and may imply a desire revert to such a state.

Crawling/walking baby

A crawling baby suggests the first stages in a new relationship or work matter. A walking baby signifies sudden independence. Numerous babies can foretell the arrival of great happiness.

Rocking a baby

Rocking a baby is linked with power. Such dreams can suggest that you are considering new work or family responsibilities, or may indicate a wish to better yourself. An attractive baby highlights prospective help from friends.

Baby crying

A dream of one's own crying baby foretells positive news. A dream of someone else's crying baby can warn against taking on other people's problems, suggesting that perhaps it's time you start looking after yourself.

POSITIVE MESSAGES

Birthday dreams often portend good luck, especially in financial or work matters. Dreaming of someone else's birthday may signify your hope that good fortune will befall that person.

NEGATIVE IMPLICATIONS

A dream that your birthday was forgotten may indicate a fear of loneliness, or a sense of being undervalued. Your dream may indicate that you feel you are not fully respected at work or at home. Perhaps you should think about how to make those around you more appreciative of you.

EMOTIONS

Birthday dreams can highlight fears of aging, and of time passing too quickly. You may be worried about the future and how you will meet the physical and emotional challenges that face older persons.

BIRTHDAY

Dreams about birthdays usually reflect optimism about the future and satisfaction with the dreamer's current state of affairs. The imagery associated with birthdays implies joviality, enjoyment, and sharing happiness with others. The dreamer's attitude toward the birthday may provide an insight into his or her true feelings about his or her present situation and future prospects. Some birthday dreams are linked to fears about aging and time moving too quickly. Others may be tinged with worry, yet also celebrate the dreamer's life and the achievements still to come.

Birthday presents

Dreams of opening birthday presents can show excitement and curiosity about the future. Think about how you felt about the presents; these emotions may describe your true feelings about the gift-givers.

Birthday cake

A dream birthday cake may demonstrate your willingness to share your life with others, or your ability to be generous with time or material objects.

Candles

Candles on a cake indicate an optimistic outlook and a lightness of being. A cake full of candles may also be linked to fears of aging and uncertainty about the future.

POSITIVE MESSAGES

A dream of your own wedding points to the cementing of a new loving relationship, and to the potential for this union to last for a long time.

EMOTIONS

If you felt positive at your dream wedding, this can indicate confidence that a loving relationship will be long-lasting. Any feelings of dissatisfaction may reveal fears that a current relationship will not endure.

NEGATIVE IMPLICATIONS

Your dream may be telling you not to try so hard in your quest for the perfect mate—you may find what you seek when you least expect it. Wedding dreams can also signify fears about becoming too involved in a relationship.

WEDDING

Dreams about weddings generally symbolize the coming together of the male and female aspects of the psyche. Consequently, they can denote a time of emotional "wholeness," when male and female energies are working together. A wedding dream can also express other forms of emotional joining. The dreamer should consider whether the wedding was specific to a particular culture or religion, and if so, what implications this could have in waking life. If the dreamer is already married, a wedding dream may be a repetition of a joyous event, or a reevaluation of his or her marriage vows. If the dreamer is not married, a dream featuring a wedding may be a form of wish fulfillment.

Wedding cake

Eating wedding cake indicates a potentially prosperous future. This may take the form of material wealth, new friendships or love relationships. Think about the flavor of the cake: was it rich and delicious, or did it leave an unpleasant taste?

White wedding

A bride in white may reveal your moral attitude—toward sex, for example. In Western tradition, white represents purity, innocence, peace, and happiness, but in parts of the East, white symbolizes mourning. If the bride was wearing a color, note its associations for you.

Bridesmaid

If you were a bridesmaid, how did you feel about the bride? Were you pleased for her—or jealous? Did you play an active part in the wedding, or did you hide from the conviviality? Did you catch the bride's bouquet?

DROWNING

Dreams of drowning usually imply that things are a struggle for the dreamer right now, and that he or she is having trouble "keeping his or her head above water." Such dreams may also denote feelings of being overwhelmed by a female figure.

POSITIVE MESSAGES

A dream of drowning, or of witnessing another person's drowning, can mean that you will overcome difficulties presently facing you.

NEGATIVE IMPLICATIONS

Drowning dreams can indicate that you feel out of control. Such dreams may suggest that swift action is needed to tackle immediate problems.

EMOTIONS

Dreams of drowning may highlight sensations of being overwhelmed by a current situation. Fears about money and future financial hardship may also be represented.

The sea

Dreams of drowning at sea can allude to feelings of insecurity and uncertainty about the future. Try to remember if land was in sight.

Swimming pool

A swimming pool setting can symbolize a secure or "contained" mental state. It may also suggest a contentment with your life.

Rescue from drowning

Saving a drowning person in a dream may symbolize the fighter in you. Or, such a dream may suggest a cry for help from someone close to you.

PREGNANCY

Pregnancy dreams are often associated with creativity and the sustaining of a new idea or project. Jung saw pregnancy dreams as symbolizing the beginning of a new phase of personal development.

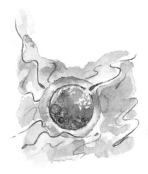

POSITIVE MESSAGES

When a woman wants to have a baby, a dream of giving birth can be a form of wish fulfillment. Many women report having had such a dream just before discovering that they are pregnant.

NEGATIVE IMPLICATIONS

When a woman does not want to have a baby, such a dream may express fears of pregnancy, of the pain of giving birth, or of parenthood itself.

EMOTIONS

For both men and women, a pregnancy dream can indicate a desire to nurture and care for someone else.

Multiple pregnancies

Dreams that involve more than one baby may indicate divided loyalties; they warn to weigh your priorities carefully, instead of trying to satisfy everybody at once.

Painful pregnancy

A painful or uncomfortable pregnancy is often connected with the demands of someone who is dependent on you. Perhaps you should consider ways of easing this burden.

A friend's pregnancy

Dreaming that a friend is pregnant indicates a deep wish for her to have a long and healthy life, and suggests a close bond between the two of you.

BAPTISM

The principal symbolism of baptism—whatever its form—is rebirth, renewal, and resurrection. Baptism dreams usually mark the end of a stage in the dreamer's emotional or physical life and the beginning of a new one.

POSITIVE MESSAGES
A baptism dream strongly suggests immersion in a new project. Or, you may be working on an initiative that will prove successful.

NEGATIVE IMPLICATIONS
Future unforeseen circumstances may bring disappointment in their wake, but you will soon find a way to get back on track.

EMOTIONS
A baptism dream can indicate a desire to become stronger and more assertive.

BURIED ALIVE

A dream of being buried alive can be terrifying. Such dreams are, however, usually the graphic expression of hidden feelings that are not necessarily alarming.

POSITIVE MESSAGES
A buried alive dream can indicate that you have successfully concluded a particular matter—you have laid it to rest.

NEGATIVE IMPLICATIONS
Such dreams were traditionally seen as omens of ill fortune, signifying difficult times ahead.

EMOTIONS
A fear of imprisonment is implied, suggesting that you feel trapped in a particular situation.

FUNERAL

Dreams of funerals are likely to be upsetting, but they deserve examination. The dreamer should consider his or her connection to the events in the dream, as well as his or her feelings toward the deceased person.

POSITIVE MESSAGES
Dreaming of attending a funeral can, surprisingly, be a sign of upcoming celebrations. Dreaming of your own funeral indicates the cessation of a specific worry.

NEGATIVE IMPLICATIONS
If you have fallen out with the deceased, the dream may express your enduring hostility.

EMOTIONS
If you felt sad in the dream, you may need to examine your feelings toward the deceased, and perhaps reevaluate your behavior toward that person.

SKELETON

The symbolism of skeletons or skulls in dreams is generally much less frightening than one might expect. They can suggest that the dreamer is reaching the heart of a complex issue.

POSITIVE MESSAGES
Dreams of museum or demonstration skeletons can foretell the arrival of new friends or colleagues.

NEGATIVE IMPLICATIONS
Skeleton dreams may show concern about a domestic problem.

EMOTIONS
Dreams that involve skeletons relate to a fear that the "skeletons in your closet" will be revealed.

POSITIVE MESSAGES

A dream of killing a person or another creature can represent positive change—getting rid of the old and bringing in the new. Some analysts see dream killing as a sign of future success in business or an enterprise.

NEGATIVE IMPLICATIONS

Some killing dreams warn of intense emotional stress. The violent nature of your dream may be an expression of extreme anger in your daily life.

KILLING

Killing dreams usually leave the dreamer with strong—sometimes terrifying feelings. Many dream interpreters argue that such dreams are an expression of envy, anger, or resentment toward an individual, group, or institution. Killing dreams are also thought to indicate the dreamer's desire to avoid dealing with some instinct, desire, or aspect of him- or herself.

Dream analysts generally agree that the repressed content of a person's unconscious, which emerges in dreams, needs to be integrated into his or her conscious life. Killing dreams can signify the need for the integration of some of the dreamer's most intense feelings. The dreamer should consider

Execution

Dreams of execution are dramatic by nature. They may reflect a sense that time is running out, and that swift action must be taken before it's too late.

Massacre

If you dream of a massacre, ask whether you are angry with yourself, or if you feel enraged about some social injustice. Explore the strength of any anger you feel, and consider how to defuse it in your waking life.

Poisoning

A dream of being poisoned might relate to your vulnerability. You may be concerned that someone bears you a grudge and intends to deceive or attack you.

EMOTIONS

Has someone or something aroused feelings of bitterness, envy, or anger in you? Try to relate your dream to recent occurrences. Think of solving any conflict diplomatically before attempting to "attack" the issue.

whether he or she was the killer or the victim in the dream; each role has different implications for emotions relating to power and vulnerability. Killing dreams can also symbolize the end of negative behavior, thoughts, and feelings.

Planning a murder

Planning a murder in a dream may indicate that you are feeling intolerant of someone or something in your waking life. If you killed someone by accident, this could be a sign that worries concerning social or work matters are unjustified.

Killing with a spear

If the dream killing is carried out with a spear or a similar ancient weapon, this may be a sign of potential danger. Such a dream may also indicate a sense of dissatisfaction with some aspect of your life.

Murder of a family member

Dreaming of a family member's murder can be connected to the idea of sacrifice. Such a dream may signify a need to give something up in order to achieve an aspiration in your waking life.

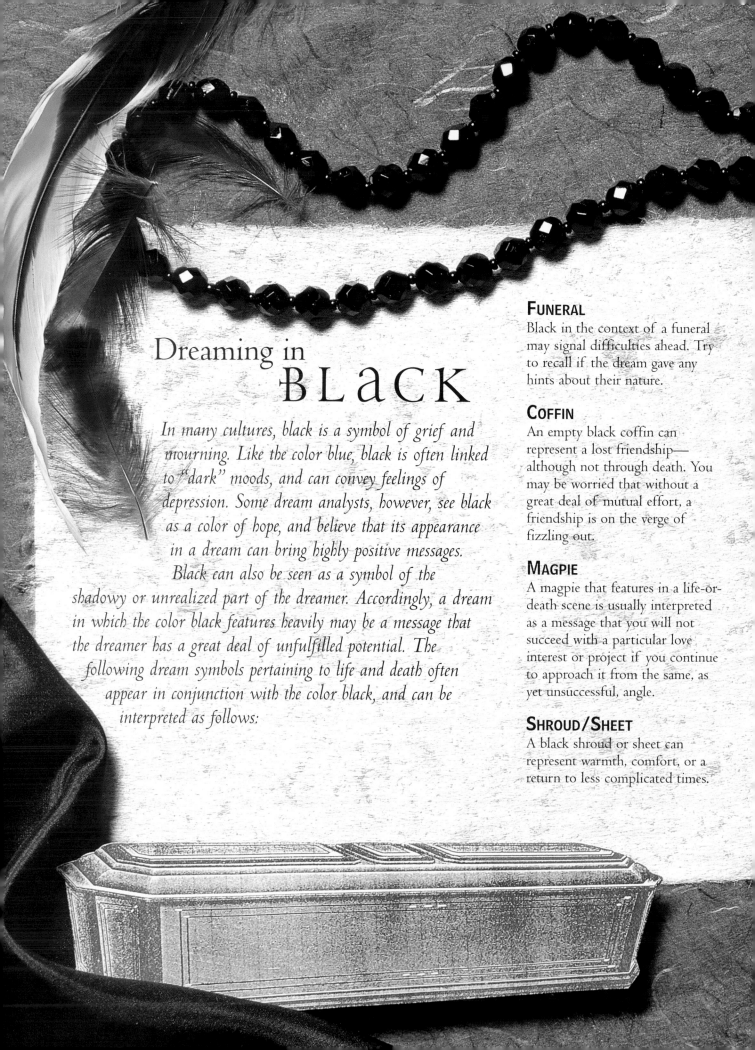

Dreaming in
BLACK

In many cultures, black is a symbol of grief and mourning. Like the color blue, black is often linked to "dark" moods, and can convey feelings of depression. Some dream analysts, however, see black as a color of hope, and believe that its appearance in a dream can bring highly positive messages.

Black can also be seen as a symbol of the shadowy or unrealized part of the dreamer. Accordingly, a dream in which the color black features heavily may be a message that the dreamer has a great deal of unfulfilled potential. The following dream symbols pertaining to life and death often appear in conjunction with the color black, and can be interpreted as follows:

FUNERAL

Black in the context of a funeral may signal difficulties ahead. Try to recall if the dream gave any hints about their nature.

COFFIN

An empty black coffin can represent a lost friendship—although not through death. You may be worried that without a great deal of mutual effort, a friendship is on the verge of fizzling out.

MAGPIE

A magpie that features in a life-or-death scene is usually interpreted as a message that you will not succeed with a particular love interest or project if you continue to approach it from the same, as yet unsuccessful, angle.

SHROUD/SHEET

A black shroud or sheet can represent warmth, comfort, or a return to less complicated times.

Other dream symbols commonly linked to the color black include:

Blackberries
Blackberries can be a sign of a setback on the way to the resolution of a particular goal.

Blackbird
Blackbirds in flight can indicate that you will be required to demonstrate great practical or moral courage in the future.

Blackboard
To dream of a blackboard with chalk marks on it can show concern about the security of your financial arrangements.

Hole/Cellar
A black hole or cellar can represent the workings of your unconscious mind.

Animal
A black dream animal can be a symbol of repressed emotions or unfulfilled aspirations.

Night
A very dark night can reveal a sense that your life lacks direction.

Necklace
A black necklace worn to a celebratory event may be a positive omen in the realm of romance.

Sheep
Dreams of black sheep are traditionally associated with temptation, envy, or greed.

FORCES OF
NATURE

*S*ome of the most vivid and
*S*dramatic dreams focus on the
fundamental forces of nature.
Dream analysts traditionally link
such dreams to the dreamer's true
emotions. The turbulent character
of many natural forces can also
represent complex situations faced
by the dreamer in waking life.

EARTHQUAKE

Earthquake dreams often signify the dreamer's perception that his or her world is in turmoil. The dream can reveal fears of instability, or concern that a major "foundation" of the dreamer's life is under threat.

POSITIVE MESSAGES

Dreaming of earth tremors can presage the arrival of a positive change, the outcome of which may be highly rewarding if you act with determination.

NEGATIVE IMPLICATIONS

The appearance of loved ones in an earthquake dream suggests that they may be experiencing some sort of crisis, and may need your help.

EMOTIONS

Note how you felt when you awoke from your earthquake dream. If you were frightened, the dream may relate to a persistent worry in your daily life.

Shaking home

If you witnessed your home shaking, the dream could indicate fears of instability in practical matters or in relationships.

Hearing the earthquake

Some analysts claim that hearing the earthquake's tremors as well as seeing its effects signifies that somebody close to you could be trying to deceive you.

Falling building

A building falling on you suggests that you are feeling the weight of your responsibilities.

VOLCANO

The tempestuous, fiery, and unpredictable nature of a volcano is usually associated with the eruption of suppressed emotions in the dreamer. Such a dream may signal the necessity of facing long-buried feelings.

POSITIVE MESSAGES

Volcano dreams can represent a massive shift in your internal world. You may be facing the realization that changing your ways is necessary in order for you to progress on your life path.

NEGATIVE IMPLICATIONS

A dormant volcano may be a warning about the reliability of new projects, and a signal to consider all options before you act.

EMOTIONS

Consider the strength of the eruption in your dream. How did you and those around you react to it?

Erupting volcano

A furiously erupting volcano can signify a potentially harmful situation of which you are unaware or which you have been ignoring.

Smoking volcano

A smoking volcano is said to symbolize passion. Note whether it was emitting great plumes, or merely wisps of smoke.

About to erupt

A volcano on the verge of eruption may signify a deep fear of someone powerful or authoritative who could stop you from completing a goal.

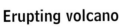

POSITIVE MESSAGES

A moderate fire burning safely in the hearth of your home can symbolize feelings of satisfaction with your personal life. If the fire burns without releasing sparks, it may signify that you are in good physical and mental health.

NEGATIVE IMPLICATIONS

In Eastern cultures, the custom of burning the dead is a symbolic purgation. If something was burned in your dream, therefore, it may represent an element of your waking life that needs to be purged. Is there something—or someone—from which you need to free yourself? Alternatively, is there an obstacle in your workplace that you need to overcome?

FIRE

Dreams about fire are frequently connected to themes of destruction and purification. The severity and heat of the fire may be direct representations of the dreamer's emotional being. The way in which the fire was handled is crucial to the dream's interpretation. An unchecked fire may be a symbol of unquenched anger, or could denote a fiery disposition. If the fire was extinguished, this can signify the suppression of physical or emotional energy. The dreamer's position in relation to the dream fire is also important. Close proximity to the flames indicates a connection with extreme emotions. Involvement in extinguishing the fire can suggest that the dreamer is in the process of

Burning home

A dream home on fire is likely to be an image of yourself. The dream may be telling you that you are in need of "cleansing," either emotionally or physically. Were you able to stop the fire from spreading—or did it engulf the entire property?

Crops on fire

Dreams of crops in flames were traditionally interpreted as a sign of imminent famine or death. In a modern—and especially an urban—context, such dreams may signify lean times ahead.

Building a fire

Building a fire—particularly if someone helps you—can presage a romantic alliance. Was your co-builder someone you recognized, or was he or she unfamiliar? When the fire was completed, were you able to contain its flames together?

EMOTIONS

Fire can represent light, spirituality, or inner power, depending on the dream's context. How did you feel about the dream fire? Were you afraid for your life, or did you feel excited or inspired by the rising flames? Dream fires can also symbolize passion and libido. Might the fire dream be connected to someone in your waking life?

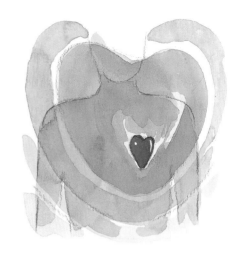

dealing with these intense feelings, whereas if the fire was viewed from a distance, such feelings may be elusive. It is also crucial to note who else was present in the dream. Did family, friends, or work colleagues help fight it?

Fire engine

A dream fire engine may be a warning that your property or loved ones need protection. If firefighters appear, this could signify a yearning for some form of adventure or excitement. Alternatively, it could mean that you are seeking a protector from something in your life that is causing you distress.

Extinguishing the fire

The ability to put out a dream fire rapidly can signify your ability to defeat adversaries in current challenges. Think about how you extinguished the fire. Did you use any equipment? How high was the fire before you managed to put it out?

Arson

A dream in which you committed arson may refer to an unexpressed rage in your life. What were you burning—and what might this object represent? Were you alone, or were others involved? How did you start the fire? Were you caught in the act?

POSITIVE MESSAGES

A calm dream ocean is often said to foretell untroubled times. It may also represent positive relations with people, especially women. Did you swim in the ocean, or just admire its tranquility from the shore?

NEGATIVE IMPLICATIONS

Engulfment by waves in your dream may denote fear of your repressed emotions and a current struggle to keep them under wraps. Being suffocated by a wave might also represent feelings of being "smothered" or oppressed by your mother or a mother figure in your life.

EMOTIONS

A dream ocean may represent your emotional life. Because water is associated with life in the womb, a dream of floating calmly in warm water may be a "comfort" dream, reconnecting you with the environment of life before birth.

⊕ OCEAN

The ocean is often interpreted as a symbol of the unconscious. Accordingly, analysis of dreams featuring the ocean tends to rely heavily on the nature of the water. Some claim that the ocean is a mother symbol—either of one's own mother or of Mother Nature. The ocean can also represent characteristics traditionally regarded as feminine, such as intuition. In mythology, the dream ocean represents power and force; the strength of crashing waves echoes the human struggle on earth. There is also a mystic tradition that the ocean is a form of "the one spirit," or a higher power.

Ocean voyage

A dream ocean voyage can predict a lucky escape in some domain of your life. The vessel in your voyage may represent your home life—look for clues, such as the boat's name or color.

Several vessels

If there were several vessels in your dream, how did they interact? How did they cope on the ocean waters? Could they survive independently, or did they need to cooperate to stay afloat?

Shipwreck

A dream of being shipwrecked suggests fears of personal or financial ruin. Note how you dealt with the shipwreck. Were you part of a salvage team? If so, what did you recover from the wreckage? If you took scant notice of the shipwreck, consider whether you are trying to avoid a problem in your life.

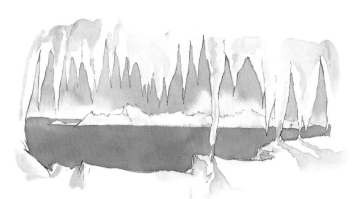

POSITIVE MESSAGES

Ice dreams occurring outside of the winter season were traditionally thought to signal a fruitful harvest. A harvest can also represent the fruition of ideas, so consider which "crops" may need your attention.

NEGATIVE IMPLICATIONS

A dream of ice may be a warning that it is time to get a project that you have put "on ice" underway. The dream may be a clarion call for immediate action.

EMOTIONS

The perception of bitter cold in a dream usually represents an emotional extreme. For example, the appearance of an icebox or freezer in your dream may reflect an emotional numbness that you are presently experiencing.

ICE

Remember that ice is made of water—and water dreams often relate to the emotional parts of a dreamer's life. The transformation of water to ice can represent the hardening of an emotion toward someone close to the dreamer. Conversely, the melting of dream ice can signify the thawing of a hostile relationship. Dreams in which ice melts can also signal the unlocking of creative energies and possibilities, foretelling that inspirational times may lie ahead at home or at work.

Sitting or walking on ice

A dream in which you sit comfortably on ice may predict enjoyable living conditions. Walking on ice can suggest the potential for financial loss unless prudent money management is applied.

Thick or thin ice

Note the consistency of the ice in your dream. A thin sheet may signal that you are being fickle in some way, while a thicker slab might imply that you feel secure even in the face of great challenges in your waking life.

Skating

Skating on ice alone suggests that you are feeling satisfied with a project you have undertaken. Skating with another person can indicate concern about a personal relationship.

SUN

Many analysts associate dreams featuring the sun with truth, power, and intellectual prowess. The sun's heat is usually linked to the emotional intensity of the dreamer's feelings. The sun can also symbolize male energy.

POSITIVE MESSAGES

A dream in which the sun rises majestically above the horizon can signify the advent of positive news. A rising sun can also represent the potential for the creation of wealth.

NEGATIVE IMPLICATIONS

A setting sun may symbolize a downward spiral in your life, and can foretell thwarted plans or ambitions.

EMOTIONS

A bright sun can be a sign of interior strength, whereas a sun shrouded in clouds may indicate personal weaknesses.

Red-hot sun

A scorching dream sun denotes the possibility of obstruction in your working life, or potential problems associated with family relationships.

Rays in the bedroom

Dreaming that the sun's rays bathe the bedroom in light is usually taken to signify financial gain.

Sun on the face

A dream sun shining on your face or head is said to denote a sense of personal satisfaction. Such a dream may also signify the belief that others respect you.

SKY

Human beings have always associated the sky with an awesome presence beyond themselves. A dream sky is therefore frequently seen as representing the height of what the dreamer wishes to achieve consciously.

POSITIVE MESSAGES

A clear sky can announce pleasurable times ahead, with no obstacles in the way. It can also foretell that a solution to a current problem will become crystal clear.

NEGATIVE IMPLICATIONS

Dreams of cloudy skies can forecast turbulent times ahead. They may also signify that you are living "under a cloud," meaning that you are carrying some sort of weighty burden.

EMOTIONS

The enormity of a dream sky can represent vast creative potential. Did you enjoy seeing your dream sky, or did you find it frustratingly out of reach?

Flying

If you were flying in the dream sky, try to understand why you were doing so. For example, were you trying to get a bird's-eye view of a problem in your waking life?

Blue sky

Some analysts believe that a very blue sky indicates that you will discover a lost or stolen item. It can also signify that a planned voyage will be successful.

Colorful sky

A colorful sky is often linked to romance. It could symbolize a current relationship—or warn of an ill-advised tryst.

LIGHTNING

Lightning in a dream can be a powerful sign and must be interpreted with caution. Some analysts argue that lightning dreams reflect the dreamer's experiences; others claim they can forecast the weather.

POSITIVE MESSAGES

Dreams in which sudden flashes of lightning appear can symbolize a bright idea or insight.

NEGATIVE IMPLICATIONS

If the dream lightning damaged anything, consider what the affected object might represent for you.

EMOTIONS

Lightning dreams are usually connected to notions of power, inspiration, and strength. Consider how long the lightning lasted, and whether it made you feel fearful or exhilarated.

STAR

Dreams of stars are typically thought to represent ambition and achievement, and can reflect the desire to reach unattained goals.

POSITIVE MESSAGES

A dream of a clear sky filled with stars is generally viewed as a sign of prosperous times or a possible future journey.

NEGATIVE IMPLICATIONS

A sky filled with pale stars can signify difficult times ahead.

EMOTIONS

Your nearness to the dream star may indicate how close you are to realizing your ambitions. Might the star be able to act as a "guiding light?"

STORM

Storm dreams are frequently interpreted as omens of difficulties or dangers that await the dreamer in waking life. Some analysts point out, however, that a dream storm can also foretell calm periods ahead.

POSITIVE MESSAGES

If you managed to find shelter from your dream storm, this may predict the positive resolution of a problem in your love life.

NEGATIVE IMPLICATIONS

Storm dreams can be directly connected to worries about obstacles presently facing you. They can also predict future complex challenges.

EMOTIONS

A short-lived storm can denote smaller problems, whereas a lasting tempest may reveal deeply rooted emotional difficulties.

HAIL

Because hailstones are cold and hard, they are often associated with determination and perseverance. The dreamer who escapes the hailstorm may thus be someone who can overcome a succession of complicated hurdles.

POSITIVE MESSAGES

Dreaming about the end of a hailstorm can herald a positive change in your creative life. Such a dream may signify embarkation on a new project or a bold work-related initiative.

NEGATIVE IMPLICATIONS

Being trapped in a hailstorm can symbolize envy or jealousy.

EMOTIONS

Consider how you dealt with the hail in your dream. Did you enjoy feeling the icy stones on your face? If so, this may indicate that you enjoy rising to challenges.

RIVER

Some see rivers in dreams as symbolizing the path of life. They can refer to the passing of time, or to the dreamer's journey from birth to death. A river can also represent the flow of emotions, and that of creative or sexual energy.

POSITIVE MESSAGES

Crossing a dream river in a vessel may represent a significant change in your life's direction. This can be interpreted positively if you are willing to embrace new developments in your waking life.

NEGATIVE IMPLICATIONS

Falling into a dream river can warn of domestic concerns on the horizon. Jumping in can signal that hasty actions are not required in connection with a pressing problem.

EMOTIONS

Try to recollect how you felt about the dream river. Did it make you feel afraid, or did it calm you?

Watching the river

Were you observing the river passively from the bank? If so, this may indicate a need for you to get in touch with your emotions.

Calm surface

"Still waters run deep" can be a truthful adage; a calm surface may belie trouble beneath your dream river.

Walking along a river bank

To dream of walking along a river bank can signify feelings of contentment with the progression of your career.

THUNDER

In ancient times, thunder dreams were associated with the voices of the gods, who were seen to be directing the dreamer with their power and wisdom. Today, dream thunder is thought to signify the conclusion of an episode in the dreamer's life. Thunder can also symbolize the release of anger.

POSITIVE MESSAGES

Hearing dream thunder close by traditionally signified a trading victory, a successful harvest, or a happy marriage.

NEGATIVE IMPLICATIONS

A thunderbolt falling when there is no storm in progress can signify a need to make a life change, or to seek solutions in previously unexplored places.

EMOTIONS

Booming thunder indicates that a problem that had been frightening you will soon be solved. Distant thunder, however, can represent problems that are "rumbling on."

Thunder over your home

Dream thunder that occurs directly above your home suggests that you are concerned about monetary loss or damage to your possessions.

Distant thunder

Hearing distant thunder in a dream may foretell that good news will arrive from a friend or relative in a distant country.

Muted thunder

Muted thunder can signify that certain friends are not what they seem, and may have befriended you for ulterior motives.

MOON

The moon governs the ebb and flow of the tides, as well as rainfall and menstruation—even birth. Aboriginal tradition holds that the moon helps women conceive. Accordingly, in dream interpretation, the moon is thought to symbolize fertility, growth, and empowerment.

POSITIVE MESSAGES

The sight of a bright moon in a dream may foretell exciting personal or career developments in the dreamer's immediate future.

NEGATIVE IMPLICATIONS

Dreaming of a moon shadowed by the sun is often interpreted as a negative omen.

EMOTIONS

Did you fly to the moon in a rocket? If so, this could express a desire to travel, or to expand your horizons.

Falling from the sky

To dream of the moon falling from the sky can depict fears about the health or safety of a close friend or family member.

Shining into your bedroom

A dream moon shining onto your bed can signify forgiveness—either from or to you. If your dream bedroom window was open, the forgiveness may come quickly.

Bright moon

To dream of a bright moon is often said to denote that the dreamer feels loved by his or her partner. Such a dream may also foretell a windfall in the near future.

PLANETS

Dreams about planets are often taken to mean that the dreamer is looking for some means of escape from his or her present earthly situation. In interpreting such a dream, the ease or difficulty of the journey should be considered.

POSITIVE MESSAGES

Dreams involving planets can suggest that you are about to embark on a significant life change—whether at work, or in social or family affairs.

NEGATIVE IMPLICATIONS

To dream about other planets may reveal an underlying sense of dissatisfaction with your daily routine.

EMOTIONS

The vast distance between Earth and other planets may suggest that you feel a need for radical change or action in your life.

Mars

Mars is named for the Roman god of war. Accordingly, dreams featuring this planet are often associated with boldness, power, and the ability to achieve one's goals.

Mercury

In Roman mythology, Mercury was the messenger of the gods. Thus, a dream in which this planet appears may be interpreted as a direct message from your inner self.

Venus

Named for the Roman goddess of love, dreams about Venus may reflect sexual desires.

Dreaming in BLUE

The color blue is thought to represent the power of the conscious mind—especially if it appears in a dream sky. It is also traditionally associated with transparency, spirituality, and infinity. Some analysts believe that the appearance of blue in a dream can indicate feelings of gentleness or patience. Different shades of blue can reflect the dreamer's present emotional state: a bright blue may suggest happiness, while a brooding indigo may foretell a downward emotional cycle. The following forces of nature often appear in conjunction with the color blue:

WATER
Blue water in a dream is often linked with the dreamer's emotional life. Vivid blue dream water can be a sign that you need to pay attention to your emotions.

HAIL
Blue hail in a dream, like falling rain, usually has emotional significance. Try to recall how long the hail lasted. If you were caught in a hailstorm, did you feel afraid or exhilarated?

AIR
A dream featuring gusts of blue air can signify a yearning for freedom in your emotional or working life.

SMOKE
If blue smoke appeared in your dream, did it obscure your view—or swirl upward to some exciting destination?

Other dream symbols commonly linked to the color blue include:

Precious stone
A blue gemstone can signify liberation from a current problem.

Clothes
Blue clothes can be a symbol of masculinity, or of the male side of your nature.

Blue bird
A blue bird may symbolize happiness, hope, and liberation.

Caged bird
A caged blue bird can signal a lack of independence and a yearning for emotional freedom.

Artwork
Blue paintings or drawings may be general reflections of your present life circumstances.

Photograph
A dream photograph tinted blue suggests that something is obscured from view in your waking life.

Heart
A blue heart may refer to a quarrel between yourself and a loved one.

Vase
A blue vase can be a sign that you feel emotionally contained.

VEGETATION AND NATURAL SURROUNDINGS

*D*reams that feature vegetation or take place in the natural arena often reflect the dreamer's life path. The potential for healthy growth in trees and plants can be linked to the dreamer's development, while the decay of vegetation can express anxiety about emotional strength or spirituality.

POSITIVE MESSAGES

Dreams that feature everyday flowers may be connected to feelings of security in your career or home life. An abundance of flowers can foretell unexpected financial satisfaction.

NEGATIVE IMPLICATIONS

If the dream flowers were arranged in a wreath, this is often associated with feelings of guilt or hostility. If you received the wreath, you may be reevaluating a relationship with someone with whom you have recently quarrelled.

EMOTIONS

The sending of flowers is sometimes linked with personal satisfaction or the need for recognition. If you received the flowers, how did they arrive? If you sent the flowers, who was the recipient—and what are your waking feelings toward that person?

FLOWERS

The everyday association of flowers with pleasure seems to carry over into dreams. Many dreamers state that dreams featuring flowers make them feel calm or reassured. Although flowers are generally viewed as positive symbols, their nature and texture can have implications for the analysis of the dream. Were the flowers freshly blooming—or were they wilting or even dead? The dreamer should consider as well whether he or she enjoyed tending or admiring the flowers, or whether they engendered regret or bitterness. Flowers are also associated with giving and love, and so it is important to reflect on the giver and the receiver of the dream flowers. Was the gesture an act of romantic love, of forgiveness, or of reconciliation?

Wildflowers

Wildflowers are sometimes associated with daring and adventure; their appearance in a dream may predict an exciting initiative in the future. Wildflowers can also be symbolic of unspoiled nature and a more relaxed approach to life, in opposition to the planned layout of a formal garden.

Tending flowers

If you cared for the dream flowers, this could suggest the need to build on current relationships. If you over-watered them, this may indicate the need for hard work to make a failing relationship "bloom."

Roses, buttercups, and orchids

Certain flowers have traditional connotations: the rose is associated with love and bravery; the buttercup with childhood; and the orchid with physical beauty and financial wealth.

TREES

Dream interpreters usually connect trees with a person's deepest unconscious. The tree's roots, hidden beneath the earth, suggest that which lies beneath a person's visible exterior. The roots can also be seen as linking the dreamer to his or her past, perhaps suggesting the need to reconnect with elements of his or her personal history.

POSITIVE MESSAGES

A healthy tree in a dream is often seen as a symbol of the potential to achieve one's goals. A fruit-laden tree is said to symbolize "rich pickings" of a financial or personal nature.

NEGATIVE IMPLICATIONS

A decaying or dead dream tree is widely interpreted as a symbol of displeasure or fear. A tree that bears rotten fruit can indicate concerns about the future.

EMOTIONS

Dream trees can symbolize your perception of the status of your personal growth. Try to recall if your dream tree was growing proud and tall or if it was lopsided.

Chopping down a tree

A dream in which you chopped down a tree suggests memories or fears relating to loss. The loss may be of a person from your life, or of an object that you once held dear.

Climbing a tree

Climbing a dream tree may express a desire to be honored. If a crowd was watching, you may be seeking recognition.

Planting a tree

Dreams involving the planting of trees can imply that however unpromising a current proposal seems, the passage of time may bring it to fruition.

GRASS

Dreaming of grass can be relevant to the outcome of future projects. Green grass—especially if growing near flower beds—can indicate success in activities connected with work or leisure. Brown or dying grass can imply disappointment, or suggest that certain projects will be much harder to achieve than originally thought.

POSITIVE MESSAGES

A dream of a well-kept lawn can pertain to an efficiently organized work project. If the lawn's edges were very neat, you may be planning to add some finishing touches.

NEGATIVE IMPLICATIONS

Overgrown grass in your dream can signify stress in your waking life. Perhaps you need to "cut back" on your activities, and spend more time relaxing.

EMOTIONS

Was the grass growing in a field, or was it a small patch? Was it green, or was it brown?

Eating grass

If you ate your dream grass, this may be a symbol of sensual pleasures. Did the grass taste good—or did it leave a bitter aftertaste?

Planting grass

Planting grass in your dream is usually associated with the desire to provide security for yourself and your family. It can also suggest that your life will be enriched, but only over a long period of time.

Making hay

Gathering grass to make hay in your dream can signify that you should act as soon as possible in some sphere to "make hay while the sun shines."

LEAVES

In dream interpretation, healthy green leaves can symbolize growth and vitality, while dying or crumbling leaves may represent a lack of energy, or the possible ending of an activity or project.

POSITIVE MESSAGES

Leaves attached to the stem of a fruit tree can be seen as symbols of good financial luck or of prudent money management.

NEGATIVE IMPLICATIONS

Leaves whirling around on a windy day may be a sign of an argument amongst members of your family that is already happening—or that is about to begin.

EMOTIONS

The position of the leaves in relation to the tree in your dream can indicate how "contained" you feel in life. Leaves growing close to a dream tree can symbolize personal satisfaction.

BRANCHES

Branches are traditionally interpreted as signs of good luck, growth, and new life. Seen as a gift from Mother Nature, the growing branch is thought to foretell luck in the dreamer's future.

POSITIVE MESSAGES

Dream branches swaying in the wind suggest that new activities or projects are ahead for you. They can also predict that your life may soon take an interesting turn.

NEGATIVE IMPLICATIONS

Broken dream branches can signify concern about personal or work-related problems.

EMOTIONS

Given their "family tree" connotations, dream branches can represent familial relationships. Were the branches growing comfortably, or were they stunting each other's growth?

HILL/ MOUNTAIN

If a hill or mountain was ascended in the dream, the ease or difficulty of the climb may be linked with the dreamer's perception of how he or she is coping with his or her journey through life.

POSITIVE MESSAGES

A dream of standing on top of a hill or mountain is a sign of pride and honor. A quick ascent can represent the ease of your personal advancement.

NEGATIVE IMPLICATIONS

Struggling up a dream hill or mountain suggests the feeling that a problem may be hard to overcome.

EMOTIONS

Did you climb your dream hill or mountain alone or did someone help you? The answer could relate to how supported you feel in your waking life.

BUSH

In Western cultures, the image of a bush is usually associated with the biblical burning bush witnessed by Moses. Accordingly, a bush in a dream may express the dreamer's wish for some sort of guidance.

POSITIVE MESSAGES

Healthy dream bushes are usually linked to notions of support, and can foretell the arrival of help from an unlikely source.

NEGATIVE IMPLICATIONS

A dream bush with little or no foliage may be a warning not to rely on good fortune alone in pursuit of a goal.

EMOTIONS

Pruning or cutting a dream bush can be a sign that a secret will soon be revealed. If someone else was doing the pruning or cutting, note how you felt about their actions.

POSITIVE MESSAGES

A dream about gathering fruit in season is frequently interpreted as a sign of personal happiness or satisfaction. Ripe fruit is also linked to the accumulation of wealth, and to plans for financial comfort in later life. If you picked fruit in the dream, this may be a signal to start saving for less plentiful times.

NEGATIVE IMPLICATIONS

Rotting fruit can be connected to the end of a chapter in your waking life that might be closing slightly ahead of time, or to a project that may be prematurely curtailed. If the fruit was ripe when picked, but rotten when it reached the ground, you may be concerned that a current undertaking will not be successful.

FRUIT

Fruit traditionally symbolizes growth, the life cycle, sexuality, and fertility. Ripe fruit specifically is often perceived as a sign of healthy growth. This growth may relate to human life itself, to an idea, or to unconscious development within the dreamer. The life cycle of the fruit from seed to decay can also be a metaphor for the various phases of human life.

The form, texture, or fragrance of some fruits—especially figs, melons, and bananas—may remind the dreamer of male or female sexual organs. Fruits that are laden with seeds are signs of fertility and new life. Dream fruit is also said to be associated with ideas of immortality; the fruit,

Apple

In Western cultures, the apple is traditionally linked to the biblical story of Adam and Eve, and thus to notions of temptation, sin, and knowledge. For a dreamer imbued with this tradition, the dream may carry such connotations. Note how you became aware of your dream apple. Were you pointed in its direction by a cunning serpent or another messenger? Or did you find it yourself?

Peach

In many Asian cultures, the peach is a symbol of immortality, and the peach blossom is linked to notions of femininity and female allure. In the West, the peach symbolizes redemption.

Fig

The fig is universally viewed as representing fertility—an idea derived from its abundance of seeds. If you ate figs in your dream, try to recall how many you ate. If you ate just one, were you satisfied—or did you want more?

EMOTIONS

Fruit is often seen as representing growth and development. Accordingly, dream fruit may symbolize the unconscious development of your inner self. Note how you dealt with the fruit in the dream. Were you reaching out for it—possibly grasping to connect with your potential for personal growth? Or were you able to pick the fruit with ease?

which is part of a continuous life cycle, is taken to represent the unending chain of life. Fruit dreams are also linked with themes of health. Ripe, juicy fruit can symbolize good health, while rotten or decaying fruit can symbolize fears of sickness in the dreamer him- or herself or in family or friends.

Eating fruit

Eating fruit in a dream can have a sexual connotation. The luscious flavors can represent sensual enjoyment and sexual satisfaction. Many interpreters link certain fruits to parts of the anatomy: melons are said to symbolize breasts; peaches, the buttocks; and a banana, the penis.

Fruit bowl

Dream fruit arranged in a bowl or on a platter can suggest future material wealth, especially if there are many varieties. Was the bowl or platter out of reach in your dream, or were the enticing fruits easily accessible?

Unusual fruit

Dreaming of unusual fruits can reveal a yearning for extra "spice" in your life. Perhaps you are seeking an adventure or a new project to counteract the monotony of your workplace. Some interpreters propose that dreams of unusual fruit can also suggest a comfortable but simple lifestyle.

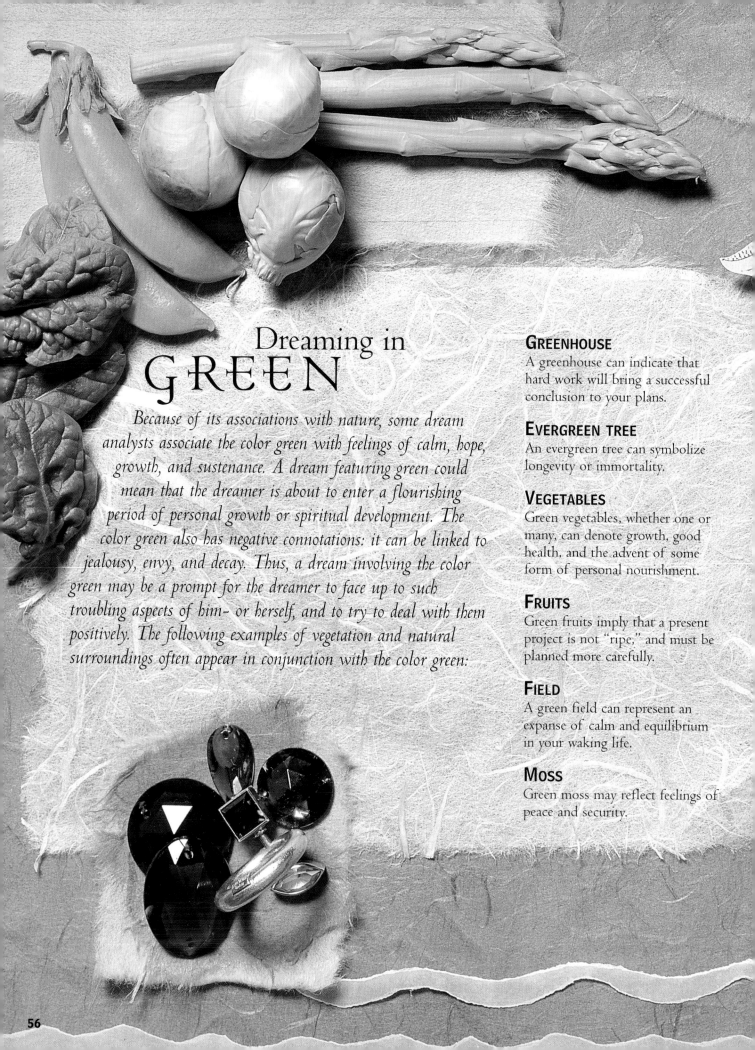

Dreaming in
GREEN

Because of its associations with nature, some dream analysts associate the color green with feelings of calm, hope, growth, and sustenance. A dream featuring green could mean that the dreamer is about to enter a flourishing period of personal growth or spiritual development. The color green also has negative connotations: it can be linked to jealousy, envy, and decay. Thus, a dream involving the color green may be a prompt for the dreamer to face up to such troubling aspects of him- or herself, and to try to deal with them positively. The following examples of vegetation and natural surroundings often appear in conjunction with the color green:

GREENHOUSE
A greenhouse can indicate that hard work will bring a successful conclusion to your plans.

EVERGREEN TREE
An evergreen tree can symbolize longevity or immortality.

VEGETABLES
Green vegetables, whether one or many, can denote growth, good health, and the advent of some form of personal nourishment.

FRUITS
Green fruits imply that a present project is not "ripe," and must be planned more carefully.

FIELD
A green field can represent an expanse of calm and equilibrium in your waking life.

MOSS
Green moss may reflect feelings of peace and security.

Other dream symbols commonly linked to the color green include:

Earthquake debris
Green earthquake debris can signify envy in a close relationship.

Flesh
Green flesh can symbolize some form of rottenness or corruption.

Green fingers
Green fingers can foretell a period of personal growth or creativity.

Eyes
Green eyes traditionally symbolize feelings of jealousy.

Gems
Green jewels or precious stones can relate to feelings of security and calmness, but may also be tied to feelings of envy.

Bills
Green bank notes can refer to a current project that involves a transaction which is being carried out from a distance.

Water
Green water can reflect feelings of stagnation, and may indicate the need to be proactive in one or more spheres of your life.

Path
A green pathway can indicate a journey of considerable distance.

PEOPLE
AND PLACES

*F*amiliar characters in
our dreams are often
associated with those who
inhabit our waking lives;
they may also signify
different aspects of our
personalities. While the
settings of our dreams
may be similarly familiar,
they can also be
symbolic—buildings, for
example, are thought to
represent our very beings.

EMOTIONS

A dream of a wedding can suggest commitment to a current relationship and a desire for it to last. Alternatively, the dream may signal a fear of commitment. Consider the emotional state of the dream bride and bridegroom. Were they radiant and excited, or fearful and unhappy?

POSITIVE MESSAGES

A dream involving a wedding couple may be mere wish fulfillment, especially if you were the bride or bridegroom.

NEGATIVE IMPLICATIONS

Some interpreters hold that seeing a bride or bridegroom in a dream can signify jealousy or rivalry.

BRIDE & BRIDEGROOM

A bride and bridegroom appearing together in a dream are often regarded as symbols of union. Their appearance can express the state of harmony or opposition prevailing in differing parts of the psyche. A dream bride or bridegroom can also represent an external union between the dreamer and another person or object.

The dreamer's role at the wedding is perhaps the most crucial factor to consider in the dream's interpretation, particularly if he or she was the bride or bridegroom or a member of the wedding party. The atmosphere at the wedding ceremony can also be telling. Was it a joyful occasion, or was it shrouded in sadness or fear?

Bride or bridegroom?

A woman's dream of a bridegroom suggests a need to get in touch with the masculine side of her personality. Similarly, when a man dreams of a bride, he may need to listen to his feminine side.

Honeymoon

If the bride or bridegroom was going off on a honeymoon, this may represent the anticipation of an imminent pleasurable event.

Your partner

If the bride or bridegroom in your dream was your current partner, you may need reaffirmation of his or her love.

POSITIVE MESSAGES

Dreams about fathers and mothers are traditionally interpreted as signs of parental love. Dreaming of your mother is sometimes said to indicate that a positive force is about to enter your life. Dreaming of your father could foretell a potential new role for you—possibly in a position of authority.

NEGATIVE IMPLICATIONS

Dreams about your parents dying can reflect current feelings of hostility toward them. Such dreams suggest that present or past conflicts are unresolved, or that problems in your relationship may lie ahead.

FATHER&MOTHER

Dreams about parents may simply express the dreamer's feelings and memories about these closest of all relatives. The meaning of such a dream can be clarified by examining the role played by the parent or parents in the dream, and the nature of the dreamer's interaction with the parental figure.

The dream father can symbolize a strong moral conscience—whether real or perceived. Childhood experiences of the father as a powerful guide and judge could be resonating in the mind of the dreamer. A dream father can also represent a figure of playfulness and affection. The dream mother can reflect the dreamer's feelings about the powerful mother—child bond. The dreamer may delight

Father or mother

A father appearing in a woman's dream indicates affection and a close bond. It may also be a signal that the dreamer should seek to develop the masculine side of her personality. The converse applies to a man who dreams of his mother.

Lying

A dream in which you lie to your parents may be a sign that you are about to complete a transaction, possibly in secret. A dream in which your parents lie to you suggests that you feel excluded from a social group.

Discipline

Dreaming of being disciplined by your parents signifies feelings of powerlessness. Think about how you might reclaim some control in your life without being too confrontational with others.

EMOTIONS

Sometimes the presence of your parents in your dreams is a straightforward representation of how you view them in your waking life. At other times, however, it is important to try to assess what messages your feelings toward your parents in your dream may hold. If your dream father is a protector, for example, this may be a prompt to become more self-reliant.

in the warmth and closeness of the relationship; or, the presence of the mother figure may symbolize a need to break away from potential over-attachment.

Important considerations in interpreting such dreams include the parental figure's behavior in the dream and the dreamer's emotional reaction to this behavior.

Crying mother

A dream of your mother in tears can be linked to your own concerns about a problem in your waking life. Some analysts believe that a crying mother signifies trouble ahead.

Benevolent father

The appearance of a benevolent father in a dream is sometimes linked to interests or hobbies in which you show only a passing interest, and which you do not intend to pursue seriously. Such a dream may be a signal for you to broaden your horizons and find a new project to take on.

Parental abandonment

Dreams in which one or both parents abandon you are usually linked to concerns about the solidity of your financial foundations. If your parent or parents eventually return, your concern is probably unfounded. If your parent or parents never return, however, this may be a signal that you need to face up to any financial problems in your waking life.

CASTLE

Dream castles tend to be associated with defense and attack, and can be a metaphor for such in personal or worldly matters. Note whether the castle was the launchpad for an attack or was besieged by enemies.

POSITIVE MESSAGES

Dreams of beautiful castles symbolize the prospect of a comfortable future, and the possibility that noble deeds will be performed.

NEGATIVE IMPLICATIONS

A castle in disrepair can warn of potential financial obstacles.

EMOTIONS

Castles, like other dream buildings, can represent yourself. Was the castle ornate, or was it still being built? Relate your answer to your personal strengths and weaknesses.

Childhood home

If the castle resembled your childhood home, it may offer clues to how you felt as a child in your parents' abode.

Cramped castle

A cramped castle may indicate feelings of frustration and a lack of opportunities.

Siege

A castle under siege suggests feelings of vulnerability and fears of being attacked.

PLACE OF WORSHIP

A dream place of worship is frequently associated with sanctuary and spiritual safety. Such a dream may also indicate a desire for some form of higher guidance in the dreamer's life.

POSITIVE MESSAGES

Dreams of participating in a religious ritual can signify joy and contentment.

NEGATIVE IMPLICATIONS

Shunning a religious building or service in your dream can be a sign of guilt over a perceived wrongdoing.

EMOTIONS

A religious building in your dream suggests that moral issues are at the forefront of your mind. You may be facing an ethical dilemma for which you are seeking guidance.

Self-worth

In ancient times, a dream of a sacred building was thought to represent the dreamer's feelings of self-worth.

Building a place of worship

Construction of a place of worship signifies the giving of presents to a loved one.

Holy person

A priest or holy person usually represents someone you respect. Consider your feelings toward that person in the dream.

DESERT ISLAND

In dream analysis, as in waking life, the desert island is an archetype of escape and isolation. The dreamer should consider whether the island inspired feelings of freedom—or fears of being marooned.

POSITIVE MESSAGES

Dreams of a desert island could be a sign that romance is headed your way.

NEGATIVE IMPLICATIONS

Being cast up on a desert island can symbolize rejection or loss of self-esteem.

EMOTIONS

For some people, desert island dreams may represent a yearning to be away from the crowd. For others, they may highlight a longing for a period of loneliness to end.

BEACH

To some people, beaches are havens of tranquility. To others, they represent a garish or empty way of life. The dreamer's reaction toward the dream beach may reflect his or her attitude toward leisure in waking life.

POSITIVE MESSAGES

Dreaming of a beach can signify escape and freedom from your daily routine.

NEGATIVE IMPLICATIONS

A beach dream can be a sign that that you are keeping a secret from someone close to you.

EMOTIONS

Think about who you were with at the beach, and what you were doing there. Were you strolling along the sand feeling elated, or were you running from dangerous waves?

FAMILIAR PLACES

Familiar places frequently appear in dreams. If a dream of home occurs when the dreamer is away and feeling homesick, it can act as a source of comfort.

POSITIVE MESSAGES

Dreams of a familiar place often represent satisfaction with the past and contentment with the present.

NEGATIVE IMPLICATIONS

Sometimes familiar dream places highlight dissatisfaction with a current situation.

EMOTIONS

Your reaction to the familiar place in your dream may reveal whether or not you have learned the lessons of your own history.

FENCE

Dreams in which a fence appears have paradoxical connotations: they can symbolize contentment or security, or denote feelings of entrapment.

POSITIVE MESSAGES

Climbing a dream fence can symbolize the overcoming of an obstacle or the realization of a goal.

NEGATIVE IMPLICATIONS

A high fence blocking your way can suggest restriction or the inability to get through a difficult situation.

EMOTIONS

A dream fence may represent feelings of being challenged or criticized. However, if you felt safe in the dream, it may signify that you feel secure in your life.

WORKPLACE

A workplace is usually associated with productivity and bustle. At times, however, it can be a place of chores and intimidation. The atmosphere of a dream workplace can be significant. Was it tense, or was there a mood of purposeful creativity? The dreamer should look for any possible connections between the dream workplace and that of his or her waking life.

POSITIVE MESSAGES
Dreams of being in your own office may predict a potential positive change in your love life.

NEGATIVE IMPLICATIONS
Dreaming that you are excluded or have been ejected from your office can denote a loss of property or of personal possessions.

EMOTIONS
Offices encompass a great deal of physical and emotional energy. Were you content or stressed in the dream office? Your feelings may have implications for your life both at work and at home.

Closed office
A closed office can indicate that something important is missing from your life.

Overcrowded office
An overcrowded office suggests feelings of being overwhelmed by too many demands.

Office problems
Dreams of office problems may signal a fear of strife entering your life.

PARK

Parks in dreams can assume a multitude of guises. The park may appear well-tended and symmetrical, or unkempt and deserted. The dreamer's reason for being in the park, the weather, and the park's location are all significant factors in interpreting such dreams.

POSITIVE MESSAGES
Park dreams are often symbolic of a sense of personal fulfillment. They can also signify feelings of freedom.

NEGATIVE IMPLICATIONS
Dreaming of a park might highlight the need for some "personal space," or a desire to escape a troubling situation.

EMOTIONS
Your feelings about the dream park can have implications for the way you organize your life. For instance, an unkempt dream park may reflect a sense of chaos in your life.

Strolling
Dreams of strolling through a park with a loved one can signal good times ahead.

Friends
Walking with friends through a park can symbolize divided loyalties.

Neglected park
A poorly maintained park may foretell a period of readjustment and possible loneliness.

CELLAR

Just as cellars and basements are situated beneath the outwardly visible part of a building, dreams about these lower levels tend to represent the hidden parts of the dreamer's inner world. Images of cellars or basements are twofold: they can be dark places full of unknown crevices, or well-lit dens of safety and play. They can also have childhood associations.

POSITIVE MESSAGES

Dreaming of a cellar or basement can indicate a journey or the possible expansion of work or business interests.

NEGATIVE IMPLICATIONS

A cellar or basement dream can express feelings of entrapment or being out of touch.

EMOTIONS

Cellar or basement dreams usually symbolize the deepest levels of your mind. Consider whether the cellar was empty or full. If full, what was being stored there?

Creatures in the cellar

Spiders and other creatures in the cellar portray fears of dealing with unexplored emotional issues.

Fuel

A cellar or basement full of coal or another fuel can be a sign that good news awaits you in the near future.

Wine

Dreams of a wine cellar may be a sign that someone close to you is preparing a deception.

STAIRWAYS

Some interpreters believe that dreams of ascending or descending a stairway have a sexual basis. Others see stairs as a symbol of general progress or ambition in life. In the latter view, the dreamer's position on the stairway signifies the degree and direction of that person's advancement.

POSITIVE MESSAGES

Stairways are thought to portray success and progress, and can highlight ambition at work or in your personal life.

NEGATIVE IMPLICATIONS

An endless stairway can signify frustration or despair.

EMOTIONS

Dreams of ascending or descending a stairway are commonly thought to be linked to deep-rooted aspects of a person's sexual self.

Spiral stairway

Spiral stairways suggest a current waking experience of "going around in circles."

Crumbling stairway

A disintegrating stairway indicates the need to establish firmer foundations in certain areas of your life.

Fire escape

Dreams of a fire escape may be a warning to remove yourself from a potentially dangerous situation.

POSITIVE MESSAGES

Dreams of building a house can denote fortuitous opportunities in work or business. Generally speaking, dreams featuring houses can reflect feelings of security about your future.

NEGATIVE IMPLICATIONS

Dreams of your house being destroyed may signal the need for changes in your daily life—changes which might entail dismantling something you have already spent time building.

H☩OUSE

Whether the dream house is a familiar or an unknown dwelling, it can symbolize the dreamer's very being. Exploring a house can signal the beginning of a journey of self-discovery, prompting the dreamer to develop some new facet of him- or herself—especially if the dream involved a familiar house, but with different rooms. Discovering a new room in the dreamer's own house could mean uncovering a new aspect of his or her personality, or it could foretell imminent change. A dream of a childhood house can express the dreamer's yearning to return to the simpler years of youth.

The existence of furniture in a dream house may reflect the dreamer's management of current

Type of house

A dream bungalow might be a warning that your life is currently being lived on just one level, either practically or emotionally. A many-storied apartment building can imply that too much is happening in your life at present, and that you need to focus more sharply on fewer areas. Dreams of tall houses can denote feelings of an "uphill struggle."

Camper/trailer

Dreams of living in a camper or trailer may suggest that it's time to "move on" in some aspect of your life, and that failure to do so will lead to emotional stagnation.

Blocked doors/windows

Impassable doors or windows highlight feelings of frustration or stifled communication. Such dreams may be a prompt for you to stand up for yourself or for some concern you hold dear. Blocked windows can represent an inability to see something for yourself; you may need to do some investigating to uncover what you seek.

EMOTIONS

House dreams are often reflections of yourself and your current emotional and spiritual state. Many analysts believe that different parts of the house represent different ages in your life. The most modern sections depict your conscious waking life, whereas the older parts symbolize the deeper layers of your unconscious. Think about how you felt in the house. Did you feel secure and comfortable, or did you feel afraid?

issues. In analyzing such dreams, the dreamer should try to recall whether the drapes in the dream house were open or closed; this might indicate his or her readiness to face current problems. The dreamer's reaction to any guests that arrive can reflect his or her real feelings toward these people in waking life.

Location of the house

The location of the dream house is often thought to be directly linked to the dreamer's current state of mind. If your dream house is situated in a quiet country backwater, this may indicate calm and tranquility in your waking life. Conversely, a house situated on a frantic, noisy street can reflect your perception of the pace of your daily life.

Brand new house

A new house in your dream is often thought to symbolize your social life. If the house has been furnished, this may foretell a busy period of socializing ahead. An unfurnished house may signify a desire to extend your circle of friends or increase your level of social interaction.

Upstairs, downstairs

The upstairs portion (attic) of a dream house is thought to represent the dreamer's intellect, and may signify the formulation or consideration of complicated or long-term plans. The downstairs portion (basement) of a house is said to represent those hidden crevices of the mind where fears and memories are buried.

POSITIVE MESSAGES

Dream kings are thought to symbolize honor, trust, and respect, and point toward a good reputation. Queens in dreams are believed to represent intuition and personal growth.

NEGATIVE IMPLICATIONS

Dreams featuring a king or a queen sometimes highlight the need to face responsibilities. They may be related to themes of authority, admonishment, and apology.

KINGS & QUEENS

Dream kings and queens can symbolize the dreamer's father and mother. Accordingly, the remoteness and power of regal figures may represent the dreamer's true feelings about his or her parents or other authority figures in his or her life. The dreamer's attitude toward the monarch in the dream is also significant. Whether the dreamer was deferential—or whether he or she revelled in a feeling of adolescent rebellion against the higher power—the dream can express a need to clarify relationships with perceived powerful figures in waking life.

Alternatively, dreams involving royalty can reflect a desire for increased status or power in the

Twin rulers

A dream in which a king and queen appear together signifies harmony in your inner life.

Chess

If your dream king and queen are chess pieces, think about their moves and who is threatened by them. A king in check may be a sign that a female figure in your life is smothering your individuality. A threat to the queen may be a warning to be wary of overbearing males.

Crown

A royal crown symbolizes a future prize that is currently just out of your grasp. However, a dream featuring the crowning of a king can be interpreted as a symbol that business or financial matters are proceeding according to plan.

EMOTIONS

Dreams of royalty tend to focus on the sensation of being a "subject." Consider your feelings of passivity in the dream, and any possible echoes in your home or work life. Were you at the mercy of the monarch, or were you able to be active? If you were the monarch, the dream could be a warning that you need to "step down from your throne" and let others have a voice.

dreamer's own life. If the dreamer was a monarch in the dream, it is important to recall how this position was attained, and also how he or she treated his or her "royal court."

King seated on a throne

A dream in which a king is seated on a majestic throne may signify a suspicion that someone is cheating you in your waking life.

Queen waving/in a carriage

A dream queen waving at a crowd from a balcony can foretell the arrival of news from a distant location. If the dream queen was riding in an ornate carriage, this may be connected to a hidden desire for power or fame—a desire of which you are ashamed.

Playing card queen

If the queen appears as a symbol on a playing card, your dream may be connected to feelings of arrogance or over-confidence. It is worth thinking before you speak or act boldly—you might regret any rash comments or deeds.

Dreaming in WHITE

In Western cultures, the color white is associated with innocence and purity. In the East, however, white is associated with death and mourning. It is thus important to note the cultural context in which the color white appeared in the dream. In a Western context, dreams featuring white can reflect feelings in the dreamer that are untarnished and pure. The appearance of white in a dream can also indicate that the dreamer's future is bright and uncomplicated. The following people and places often appear in dreams together with the color white, and can be interpreted as follows:

ROYAL PERSON

A white royal family member can be a symbol of hope. Consider whether an authority figure has recently offered you encouragement.

WOODS/FOREST

A forest or woods filled with white trees can signify a desire to enter a new, positive phase of life.

COOK/CHEF

A cook or chef dressed in white may suggest that you need "pure" nourishment, love, and affection from those around you.

ROOM

A white room can indicate a current state of tranquility.

Other dream symbols commonly linked to the color white include:

Stage

A white stage or podium can relate to success in public affairs.

Hand

A white hand may symbolize a new or improving personal relationship.

Clothes

White clothes suggest that you will be successful in current undertakings.

Sky

A white sky can express wishful thinking in some sphere of your waking life.

Bird

A white bird—particularly a dove—symbolizes peace. It may represent a desire to end personal or societal conflicts.

Building

A white building suggests that you expect to be rewarded for present endeavors.

Flower

A white flower can symbolize simplicity and purity in some aspect of your life.

Book

A white book may denote that you are laying the groundwork for a successful enterprise.

Water

White dream water can relate to purity and the need for cleansing in your emotional or personal life.

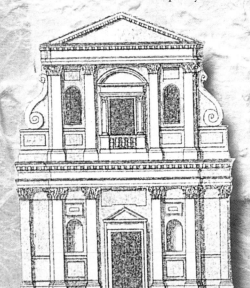

THE HUMAN BODY

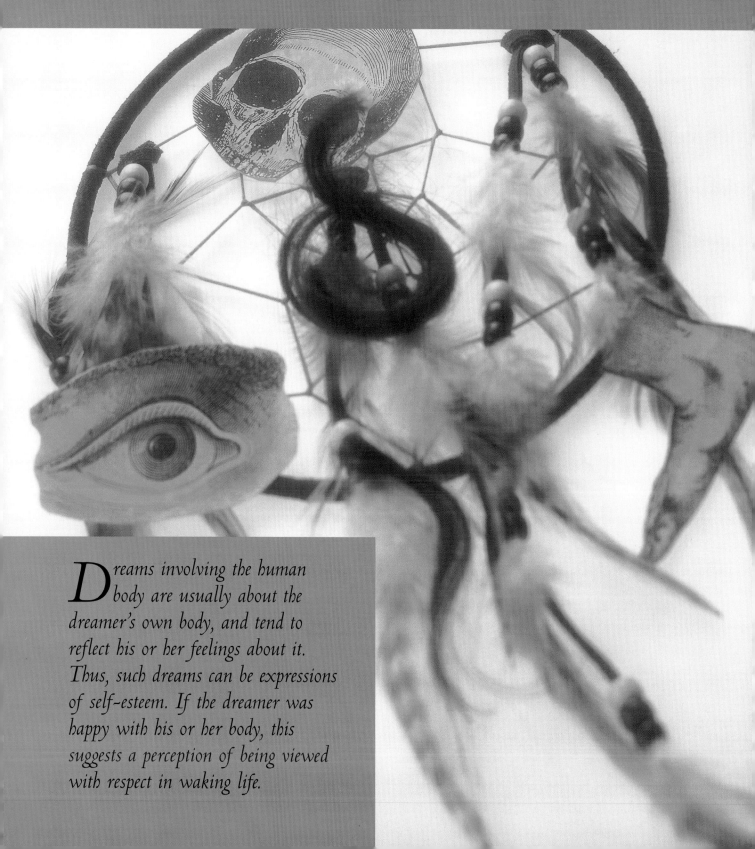

*D*reams involving the human body are usually about the dreamer's own body, and tend to reflect his or her feelings about it. Thus, such dreams can be expressions of self-esteem. If the dreamer was happy with his or her body, this suggests a perception of being viewed with respect in waking life.

BREASTS

Breast dreams are often sexual in nature, but can also relate to maternal feelings and relationships. Such dreams may denote a desire for psychological or emotional nourishment.

POSITIVE MESSAGES

Dream breasts are often connected with nature and growth. They may signify that you are undergoing a period of personal development, spiritual enlightenment, or inner healing.

NEGATIVE IMPLICATIONS

The breasts in your dream can represent an excessive attachment to a particular person—usually to your mother or to a maternal figure.

EMOTIONS

Dream breasts can symbolize Mother Earth. Do you feel you have room to grow within "your world?"

Resting head

A dream of resting on someone's breast suggests the potential to form a new and long-lasting friendship.

Voluptuous or small breasts

Full dream breasts can be interpreted as a sign of good times to come. Conversely, small or wrinkled dream breasts may foretell a future hardship of some kind.

See-through clothes

If a woman dreams that her breasts are revealed through her clothes, this may signify a sense that someone is currently admiring her.

BUTTOCKS

Buttocks appear frequently in dreams. A dream of kicking one's own buttocks can signify that the dreamer is experiencing disapproval from some source. Buttocks that are whipped may reveal a conscious or unconscious sexual appetite.

POSITIVE MESSAGES

A dream of kicking someone in the buttocks can be a sign that you are hoping for a promotion at work.

NEGATIVE IMPLICATIONS

Aiming to kick someone's buttocks, but missing, can signify that a project may fail unless you stick strictly to your plan.

EMOTIONS

If the dream is obviously sexual, consider whose buttocks were featured—and try to make a connection with your waking sexual desires.

Animal buttocks

The appearance of animal buttocks in a dream can be an omen of wealth.

Several pairs of buttocks

A dream involving several pairs of buttocks can foretell pleasant social events ahead.

Naked buttocks

Naked buttocks that you wish were covered can signify feelings of shame or guilt.

POSITIVE MESSAGES

A dream in which you are having a blood transfusion can indicate that you are on the verge of solving a current problem.

NEGATIVE IMPLICATIONS

The loss of blood generally refers to a deterioration of physical, spiritual, or moral strength. If the blood flowed from a wound, you should be wary of tentative work projects or business proposals.

EMOTIONS

Circulating blood in a dream can be an important symbol. If your dream blood moved through arteries or veins with ease, this may signify that you feel you are on the right life path. Any blockage could represent perceived obstacles to your life plan.

BLOOD

A frequent dream symbol, blood is often said to represent life itself. It is also generally related to personal strength, spiritual matters, and rejuvenation. The rejuvenation may be a form of physical recovery, of emotional awakening, or of spiritual rebirth. The intense red of blood and its role as a life force also gives it connotations of passion, love, and anger. A dream of rich crimson blood, flowing freely, can symbolize the dreamer's intense passion for a person or a situation. It can also suggest unconscious feelings of anger toward someone close to the dreamer in waking life.

Blood on the hands

Blood on your hands in a dream—an image most powerfully conveyed by Shakespeare's *Macbeth*—can relate to deep-seated guilt about an action or sphere of your life.

Hemorrhage

A dream of gushing blood can mean that you feel drained in some way. Perhaps you are in need of greater personal fulfillment—or simply a change of scene.

Bloodstained clothes

Bloodstained clothes in your dream may be a sign that someone wishes to impede you at work or to hinder your ability to pursue a fulfilling career.

POSITIVE MESSAGES

A dream of having many ears can indicate that you feel liked or respected by colleagues at work. You "have the ear" of those around you, and your opinions are often acted upon.

NEGATIVE IMPLICATIONS

Dreaming that you possess the ears of a strange or wild animal is said to symbolize the fear that someone is deceiving you.

EMOTIONS

Ear dreams can be about listening to others—or possibly, to your unconscious. Were the ears content to receive the dream information, or did they want to listen to something else? What message did the ears hear—and did it have any connection with your waking life?

Ears

Dreams about ears are usually linked to the human capacity for listening, and can relate to the dreamer's waking need to listen to the words of others. Ears in dreams can also be a warning to heed the advice of a close friend or relative, or a sign to respond to praise or criticism when it is offered. It is important to note who the ears belonged to in the dream. If they belonged to someone else, the message that they heard—and the question of whether the dreamer could hear this message as well—may have significance for the dreamer in waking life. Dreams involving ears can also suggest a fear on the part of the dreamer that somebody is withholding important information from him or her in waking life.

Ear size

The size of the dream ears can be significant. Exceptionally large ears can imply that assistance may come from an unexpected person, while small ears may suggest that you will discover that a colleague or friend has been untrue.

Washing ears

A dream involving the washing of your ears is generally interpreted as a sign that good news may be forthcoming. If you washed your own ears, you may be the bearer of the glad tidings; if someone else washed them, the good news may come from others.

Pulling ears

A dream in which your ear is pulled—or you pull someone else's ear— may signify a dispute in the workplace. How fiercely was the ear pulled? Try to relate this dream to your current work situation.

HAIR

Healthy and well-groomed hair—especially when it has a strong sheen—denotes youth, vitality, and the projection of a positive self-image. Hair that is in poor condition, or falling out, can be a sign of low self-esteem. Hair is also a symbol of sexuality. In men, it is connected with notions of virility; in women, it is associated with attracting a partner.

POSITIVE MESSAGES
Dreaming of an unfamiliar woman with beautiful hair is often associated with friendship and happiness.

Perfumed hair
Dreams of perfumed hair can be connected to arrogance or vanity. Did you apply the perfume to your hair yourself—or did someone else do so for you?

NEGATIVE IMPLICATIONS
Tangled or braided dream hair can signify complex problems in your life. Dream hair that is unmanageable may mean that you should rethink current problem-solving strategies.

Cutting hair
Having your own hair cut can signify that you will be successful in a new undertaking. Cutting the hair of another may be a warning to heed those who appear hostile toward you.

EMOTIONS
If your dream hair is well cared for, your inner self may be similarly thriving. If you have let your dream hair go, however, you may be failing to satisfy your inner needs.

Combing hair
Combing your own dream hair can relate to personal problem-solving; combing someone else's hair can denote that solutions to difficult problems lie ahead.

TEETH

Dreams of teeth usually relate to notions of self-worth. A dream of teeth falling out may be linked to the dreamer's fear of growing old, or to anxiety about his or her self-image. Rotten dream teeth can represent the deterioration of a close relationship.

POSITIVE MESSAGES
Gleaming or attractive dream teeth can symbolize wealth or friendship. A straight row of teeth may indicate harmony within a family group or friendship circle.

Pulling teeth
A dream of pulling out one or more of your own teeth is thought to be a warning: do not act until you have considered a problem from all angles.

NEGATIVE IMPLICATIONS
If one tooth is considerably larger than the rest in your dream, you may be anxious about the possible advent of sad news or a work-related disappointment.

Cleaning teeth
The cleaning of dream teeth is often connected with the giving of money to friends or relations.

EMOTIONS
Dreams involving the roots of teeth can refer to the stability of your waking relationships. If dental attention is needed, certain relationships may be in imminent need of reevaluation.

Object caught in teeth
An obstruction dislodged from the teeth can signify that a seemingly intractable problem might soon be solved. If the blockage cannot be removed, the problem may take a long time to resolve.

LEGS

A dream involving legs can reflect the extent to which the dreamer feels supported in his or her waking life, or whether he or she feels in need of some type of "crutch."

POSITIVE MESSAGES

A dream featuring strong, healthy legs implies a general sense of contentment both at home and at work.

NEGATIVE IMPLICATIONS

If you had a wooden leg in your dream, you may feel overly reliant on some form of external assistance.

EMOTIONS

Itchy legs may be a sign that a worry about a current concern is a waste of your time and energy.

SPINE

Dreams about the spine are linked with the human will, and represent the capacity for determination, courage, and self-belief. The formation of the spine can affect the meaning of the dream.

POSITIVE MESSAGES

A straight, strong, and well-formed spine can signify inner strength and determination.

NEGATIVE IMPLICATIONS

A curved or bent spine may reveal a lack of will, and can imply that you need to stand up for yourself at work or at home.

EMOTIONS

The straightness of your dream spine can reflect the degree to which you feel united with your unconscious.

FEET

Dream feet are thought to represent progress in the dreamer's life, especially if they are walking forward. Dream feet walking backward, however, may signify that the dreamer is heading in the wrong direction in waking life.

POSITIVE MESSAGES

The bathing of your feet—by yourself or another—in a dream can mean that you have distanced yourself from everyday worries.

NEGATIVE IMPLICATIONS

A dream of many feet walking together is said to signify potential material loss. Such a dream could be a warning to attend to your financial situation.

EMOTIONS

The strength or determination of the feet may indicate how you are approaching a task. Do you feel that a present goal will be a "walkover"—or will it require hard work?

HANDS

Dream hands often act as guides for the dreamer in waking life. A delicate dream hand may indicate a particular direction, whereas a weathered hand may point an entirely different way.

POSITIVE MESSAGES

The caressing of hands in a dream usually implies friendship or romance—sometimes even marriage. If you stroked someone's hand, consider that person's significance in your waking life.

NEGATIVE IMPLICATIONS

Dirty dream hands can be a warning to curb bad behavior or others will think less of you.

EMOTIONS

The dexterity of dream hands can be linked to personal matters. Were they easy or hard to manipulate? If hard, did you feel frustrated, or did you patiently persevere?

POSITIVE MESSAGES

Dreams that involve sharp sight are generally interpreted as positive omens. Clarity of vision can represent success in self-imposed challenges. Your dream may imply that a business project or career change will benefit from some "clearsighted" planning.

NEGATIVE IMPLICATIONS

A dream that your own sight is troubled or clouded is thought to symbolize the need for financial assistance. A business project may not succeed unless it is revisited at the "drawing board" stage, but if appropriate modifications are made, it stands a chance of success.

EYES

In ancient times, the eyes were said to symbolize faith. Eyes were also thought to be windows to the soul, revealing the true nature of their owner's psyche. In dreams, the eye's ability to perceive was believed to mirror the dreamer's understanding of the world. Thus, clear eyes revealed strength and vision in the soul of the dreamer, whereas eyes without sight indicated a lack of insight. These interpretations persist today, and eyes are still frequently seen as symbols of an individual's perceptions and interpretations of the world. Dream eyes are also believed to be a conduit to the future, with the ability to predict events through clairvoyant vision. The warmth or coldness of

Eye injury or disease

Dreaming of an eye injury or disease can express fears concerning your reputation. Are you are worried that someone is questioning your good character or plotting against you? Consider whether such a threat exists—and if so, whether something can be done about it.

Eyebrows

Dream eyebrows—especially shapely or attractive ones—can be symbols of dignity and honor, and may foretell the garnering of respect by an unexpected group of people. A dream of hair loss from the eyebrows can signify a loss of social standing.

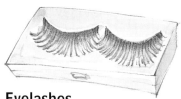

Eyelashes

A dream featuring one or more eyelashes may be connected with a secret that was shared with you—possibly a compromising revelation that would cause difficulties if passed on.

EMOTIONS

Your dream eye or eyes may be prompting you to take heed of a message from your unconscious. Note the quality and content of the dream in which the eye or eyes appeared. Were you excited by the vision in the dream? Any associations with the dream eye—however obscure they may seem—can be important channels to your unconscious.

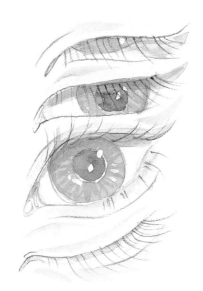

dream eye expressions is sometimes linked to the dreamer's emotional well-being. If the eyes are smiling, the dreamer may be experiencing—or about to enter—a period of contentment in waking life. If the eyes appear worried, this may reveal the dreamer's fear of emotional or psychological isolation or deprivation.

Floating eyes

Eyes that are disconnected from a face can denote an upturn in your financial situation. A floating eye or eyes may reveal a secret desire to take a risk in monetary matters. Extreme caution is needed with regards to any such venture.

Eye shape

The shape of the eyes in a dream can be significant. If they are wide and open, this may represent innocence or childlike excitement. If they are narrow or slitted, this may carry connotations of deceit.

Eye color

The lightness or darkness of dream eyes can be significant. Pale eyes may foretell a social relationship that will bring much happiness. Darker eyes tend to be linked to love interests, and may signify that you are ready—or almost ready—for a new romantic involvement.

POSITIVE MESSAGES

A beautiful dream face with no resemblance to your own can symbolize pride and honor. This meaning is enhanced if the face was smiling or appeared content. To see your own face in a mirror may foretell long, healthy lives for you and your loved ones.

NEGATIVE IMPLICATIONS

Dream faces can be familiar—or unrecognizable. An unknown face in your dream can symbolize potential changes in your life. Think about changes that may be looming on your horizon—a move to a new home or a new development at work, for example.

FACE

A dream that features a human face is thought to be linked with the dreamer's self-image, and the image—real or perceived—that the dreamer projects to others. The human face is usually the first and most significant part of a person's body to be noticed by others, and therefore conveys our image most powerfully to the outside world. The dream face can thus reflect how the dreamer wishes to be seen. If it is bright and has clear, fresh skin, this could be a true image of the dreamer—or a wishful one. A haggard face can signify that the dreamer is unhappy about his or her image in the eyes of others. The condition of the dreamer's face can also reflect his or her daily routine in waking

Familiar faces

A multitude of familiar faces can be a sign of a forthcoming celebration or social event—possibly one that you have already planned. Were the faces from the same family or friendship group, or did they represent several areas of your life?

Lips

Prominent lips on a dream face are generally interpreted as a symbol of the female genitalia. They can also be linked with communication and self-expression, and may signify the need to be more direct with persons close to you.

Mouth

Dream mouths can have similar sexual meanings to those of the lips, but they are also connected with notions of nourishment. Was the mouth smiling or frowning? This can indicate how nurtured or loved you feel at the present time.

EMOTIONS

Cleansing your face in a dream can symbolize feelings of guilt and repentance for sin. Consider whether you feel bad about something you did recently—and if so, what steps you can take to ease your conscience.

life. Was it showing the effects of a hectic schedule? A dream in which someone else's face features prominently can reflect the dreamer's feelings toward that person in waking life.

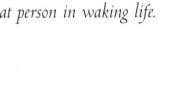

Aged face

Dreaming of a wrinkled face may simply be a representation of an older person in your life. However, such an image is also said to symbolize longevity and wisdom; your dream may be a sign that you are seeking guidance in your waking life.

Nose

A dream in which your nose is the focus can signify that you possess a greater social circle than you realize. Blowing your dream nose can foretell an increase in personal or family tasks that will bring satisfaction. A blocked nose can reveal that your plans face opposition.

Beard

Beards in dreams are often interpreted as symbols of masculinity. They can also be connected to the female side of a man's character—especially if the mouth is visible.

Dreaming in RED

With its connotations of fire, heat, and blood, the color red is usually connected with energy, vitality—and anger. The appearance of the color red in a dream can suggest passion about a project or relationship in the dreamer's current life. Alternatively, it can denote unconscious feelings of rage toward a person or situation. The color red often appears in conjunction with the following aspects of the human body:

HEART
A red heart can reveal deep-rooted passion or sexual energy that you are presently experiencing in waking life.

RASH
A red rash tends to indicate current feelings of irritation or embarrassment about a situation in waking life.

EARS
Brightly shining red ears can point to sensations of guilt, shame, or embarrassment.

Nose
A red nose can refer to current feelings of curiosity, or perhaps to a "nosy" desire to delve into the affairs of others.

Other dream symbols commonly linked to the color red include:

Flames
Red flames can indicate a perception of imminent danger. Such a warning should be heeded.

Wine
Red wine can denote richness, personal satisfaction, or happiness.

Balloon
A red balloon can symbolize your uniqueness and the feeling that you stand out from the crowd.

Paper
Red paper may be connected to the loss of a friendship.

Wedding dress
A red wedding dress, as worn by brides in the Hindu tradition, can symbolize life itself.

Rose
A red rose can be a straightforward symbol of romance and eternal love.

aNIMaLs

*T*he animals in our dreams have long
been endowed with rich symbolic
meanings. Freud claimed that they often
represent authority figures, including
parents. Dream animals may also be linked
to some primitive instinct or "inner beast"
that resides within the dreamer, but is
repressed in waking life.

BULL

The aggression and strength of a bull is often associated with masculinity. Accordingly, dreams about bulls may express an innate desire to discover the masculine aspects of the self—or to avoid them. Jung argued that the bull represented a person's true nature, and that the concomitant animal instincts were hidden behind the multiple layers of consciousness.

POSITIVE MESSAGES

A dream bull can represent an important figure in your life.

NEGATIVE IMPLICATIONS

An attacking bull in a dream can be a warning that someone you regard as a friend may be talking about you behind your back.

EMOTIONS

Bull dreams often focus on the harnessing of the creature. The ability to do so may convey how well you can integrate the "animal" aspects of your personality.

Sacrifice/Bull in china shop

The sacrifice of a bull indicates a past or future victory. The image of a bull in a china shop suggests the need to be honest with yourself in choosing suitable life options.

Bull fighting bull

Two bulls fighting can reveal disharmony among siblings— whether declared or underlying. Consider your position in the fight, and whether you were able to influence the outcome.

Bull fighting human

Such a fight may forecast the need for action to resolve an annoying facet of your personal life.

FOX

Foxes are generally regarded as sly, cunning creatures. Accordingly, their appearance in dreams can be a signal from the dreamer's unconscious that such aspects of his or her personality need to be addressed. Alternatively, a dream fox might represent a figure from the dreamer's waking life.

POSITIVE MESSAGES

Chasing, capturing, or killing a fox in a dream can signify plans to outwit those who may be plotting against you.

NEGATIVE IMPLICATIONS

Fox dreams are traditionally seen as harbingers of danger— especially hidden danger. Such a dream may alert you to be on your guard.

EMOTIONS

The sly nature of a dream fox may represent the "crafty" aspects of your character. Such a dream could be a warning to be more open in your dealings with others; or conversely, a prompt to be a bit more wily.

Tame or wild

A fox in your home environment can indicate relationship difficulties. A fox that is seen in the distance may point to a betrayal of confidence.

Fox hunting

A dream of riders hunting a fox may foretell an upcoming social engagement, or an enjoyable interaction with others.

Fox cubs

Dream fox cubs are thought to represent the warmth and coziness of the home.

POSITIVE MESSAGES

As in mythology, cats in dreams are associated with fertility and the prospect of new beginnings. Cat dreams can also foretell personal or monetary good luck.

NEGATIVE IMPLICATIONS

A cat that is killed or chased away in a dream may be construed as an omen of potential bad luck. A scratching cat can symbolize the desire to defend your territory, especially if you are feeling threatened by someone.

EMOTIONS

If your dream cat was calm, future prospects look promising. If the cat was angry or hostile, it may represent a negative or "catty" aspect of your personality. Cat dreams are also interpreted as evidence of intuition, independence, and an aura of femininity.

cat

Cats are commonly seen as symbols of wisdom, cunning, and good luck. Some believe that they even hold the mystery of life, death, and rebirth. The meanings of cat dreams can vary according to the dreamer's waking relationship with the feline creatures. If the dreamer is afraid of cats when awake, a cat in a dream may symbolize fears about certain aspects of him- or herself. If the dreamer is a cat lover, however, the cat in the dream may reflect his or her personal strengths. Cats are also thought to represent the feminine side of human nature. Thus, some analysts believe that a frightening cat dream can indicate a fear of things female.

Cat's eyes

A cat's eyes can signify finding your way through a knotty problem, or the discovery of light in a dark situation.

Meowing cat

A meowing or screeching cat is often thought to be a sign that someone is talking about you behind your back. Such a dream may highlight feelings of insecurity about friends or co-workers. Think about the noise and your reaction to it. Did you have the courage to approach the cat, or were you scared off by the sounds it made?

Nine lives

The impression of your dream cat having nine lives is connected to the overcoming of multiple obstacles. The resilience of this "survivalist" cat may represent your own inner strength and tenacity in the face of adversity.

NEGATIVE IMPLICATIONS

Fearing your dream horse may signify anxiety about the imminent loss or misplacing of an important object. A tethered horse can represent a part of yourself that needs liberating.

EMOTIONS

The dream horse's speed can reflect your feelings about the current pace of your life. A steady pace indicates that your life is traveling with the momentum you expect, while a cantering horse signifies the need for swifter action.

POSITIVE MESSAGES

Horse dreams are generally seen as indicative of contentment, and are believed to occur in people who are at ease with themselves and their surroundings.

H O R S E

Horses are traditionally associated with movement, freedom, and strength. Accordingly, horses in our dreams are thought to symbolize animal instincts that could help the dreamer to "ride away." It is important that the dreamer assess his or her relationship to the horse: who was in charge? Did the dreamer lead, ride, or follow the horse? If on horseback, did the dreamer grasp the reins tightly for fear of losing control, or was it relatively easy to steer the creature in the chosen direction?

The horse is also said to symbolize the unconscious. In certain mythologies, horses speak in a human voice. If a dream horse speaks, its words may be a message from the dreamer's inner self.

Angry horse

A bucking horse warns of possible resistance to your plans, and could indicate the need to spend more time persuading others. Fighting horses imply tension among a group of friends.

Mounting/Galloping

A rider mounting a horse in a dream may show a potential for newfound prosperity. Galloping or racing horses are portents of speedy success at work; they can also denote feelings of elation, and may represent the need to "ride above" the minutiae of the daily routine.

Horseshoe/Grooming

Horseshoe dreams are often associated with good fortune. The grooming of a horse may indicate the potential for luck in a speculative venture.

POSITIVE MESSAGES

Dreams about birds are traditionally viewed as harbingers of good fortune. Birds with outstretched wings reveal a sense of freedom, and point to a future of unlimited possibilities. If you are the flying bird, look carefully at your bird's-eye view. Is the ground clearly visible, or is it hard to see where you are heading?

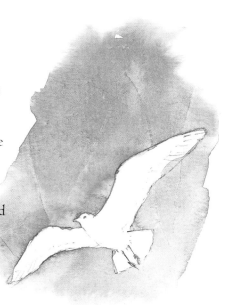

NEGATIVE IMPLICATIONS

Birds in flight can allude to a desire for escape. If the dream bird cannot fly, you may be feeling trapped in a difficult or demanding situation. A broken or clipped wing may denote that something is holding you back or blocking your path to success.

BIRD

In many traditions, the bird symbolizes both the soul and the conscious mind. Accordingly, a dream bird can signify that the dreamer's unconscious and conscious are attuned. A bird in a dream may also symbolize some aspect of the dreamer's inner world that can bring healing and wholeness. Bird dreams often leave the dreamer with feelings of exhilaration or empowerment.

In many mythologies, birds were linked with spiritualism and shamans; the bird flying above the human world could contact the gods and form a connection between the earth and the heavens. In a dream context, this could be interpreted as the dreamer's unconscious relaying an important message

Albatross/Peacock/Swan

An albatross in a dream foretells a weighty burden in need of immediate attention. A peacock is a sign of pride and satisfaction; its colorful and majestic plumage parades a personal achievement. The grace of a swan can allude to your ability to accomplish tasks smoothly and efficiently.

Ostrich/Owl/Eagle

A dream ostrich represents the avoidance of a trying situation or event; by burying its head in the sand, it refuses to face reality. An owl points to wisdom, perhaps your own, or to the need to seek counsel from a wise acquaintance. An eagle symbolizes leadership and the ability to motivate others.

Wounded bird

An injured bird in a dream portends worries which may be short-lived. If you tend to a wounded bird, this may be a sign that the generous, caring side of your personality is currently active. If the injured bird is left to fend for itself, this may signify the neglect of these benevolent aspects of yourself.

EMOTIONS

A single dream bird indicates feelings of independence and personal strength, whereas a flock of birds can reveal emotions connected to working or sharing with others. If you were part of a flock, consider your relationship to the birds in it. Were you their leader, an integral member—or were you flying behind?

or solution to a problem. A bird in a flock can carry meanings about the dreamer's interaction with others.

Vultures, crows, and ravens in dreams are often associated with death, and can imply fears about one's own death and about the death of loved ones. A blackbird is sometimes thought to represent the feminine aspects of the psyche.

Pheasant

A pheasant in a dream is generally taken to indicate good fortune in the near future. The appearance in your dream of game pheasants that have been shot and killed during a hunt can mean that your self-esteem is on the rise, or that some honor or privilege is about to be bestowed upon you.

Nightingale

A nightingale is often interpreted as a positive omen, signaling future success or possible financial gain. If a nightingale appears in your dream when you are ill, this can signify that a swift recovery will follow. If the nightingale is singing in your dream, a promotion at work may be in the pipeline.

Stork

Dreams of storks are usually interpreted as harbingers of change in the dreamer's waking life. If the stork is in its nest, this can signify that problems may arise within your immediate family.

DOLPHIN

Dolphins are usually associated with intelligence, communication skills, grace, and playfulness. The appearance of a dolphin in a dream therefore suggests that these qualities are current preoccupations of the dreamer in waking life.

POSITIVE MESSAGES

The appearance of a dolphin in a dream can be considered a sign that your intellect is being exercised, and that you are meeting cerebral challenges successfully.

NEGATIVE IMPLICATIONS

Dolphin dreams are sometimes interpreted as indicators of present unhappiness, and of the need to move swiftly on to new challenges.

EMOTIONS

Dreams of dolphins are often connected to communication—or its absence—in your life, and might relate to your unconscious trying to "get in touch" with your conscious self.

Leaping dolphins

Dolphins diving in and out of water represent successful management of the different aspects of your life.

Cold water

Dolphins swimming in cold water may signify the need to change the way you are presently handling a certain task or duty.

Warm water

Dolphins swimming in warm water may be seen as a sign of contentment with your current situation.

FISH

Jung believed that because fish are cold-blooded and are ancient participants in the earth's evolutionary history, they may symbolize a deep level of unconsciousness. Fish dreams, therefore, can be indicators of deep-rooted wishes and fears that have not yet been consciously acknowledged.

POSITIVE MESSAGES

Many fish in a dream can symbolize fertility, or that good fortune lies ahead.

NEGATIVE IMPLICATIONS

Fish in one's dreams may represent greed or the hankering after material possessions, possibly at the expense of the spiritual elements of life.

EMOTIONS

To witness many fish in a dream can represent some form of encounter with your true self. Think about how the fish were swimming, and whether you were part of the school.

Clear water/Dead fish

Fish in clear water are portrayed in some myths as omens of financial well-being. Dead fish, on the other hand, are often said to represent disappointments or failures.

Fishing

Dreaming of a fishnet may indicate a fear of being found out. Fishing can also symbolize the notion of catching repressed feelings and bringing them to the surface.

Variety of fish

A variety of dream fish can signal an increase in social or commercial activity.

MOUSE

Mice are generally thought to be timid creatures, although they can also be portrayed as devious or cunning—in the TOM AND JERRY cartoons, for example. Consider whether the dream mouse or mice were hunters or prey.

POSITIVE MESSAGES
Dreaming about a mouse may mean that you will receive some good or promising news shortly.

NEGATIVE IMPLICATIONS
A dream featuring a mouse may be interpreted as an indicator of discord among your family or a group of friends.

EMOTIONS
The overriding feelings associated with mice are timidity, embarrassment, and powerlessness. A mouse dream can therefore reflect a quest for increased emotional strength.

RABBIT

Rabbits are associated with fertility and sexuality. Like other fertility symbols, the rabbits of dreams are often interpreted as harbingers of personal growth and development, or as portents of a new project.

POSITIVE MESSAGES
A dream that centers on the eating of a rabbit can signify that you will enjoy your work and succeed at it.

NEGATIVE IMPLICATIONS
Many rabbits in your dream can represent fears about potential enemies who may try to undermine you.

EMOTIONS
A dream rabbit can symbolize the advent of responsibilities that you will be happy to take on.

SNAKE

In the Judeo-Christian tradition, the snake symbolizes evil—the serpent in the Garden of Eden, for example. In Greco-Roman mythology, the snake represents the god of medicine.

POSITIVE MESSAGES
To dream of attacking or killing a snake is associated with overcoming those who wish to see you fail.

NEGATIVE IMPLICATIONS
A coiled snake can indicate danger or that you feel restricted in some way.

EMOTIONS
Snake dreams can highlight your innate wisdom or your sexuality. They can also signify deep-rooted temptation or jealousy.

TIGER

The power and cunning associated with tigers may symbolize a person or situation that has been frightening or confusing the dreamer in waking life.

POSITIVE MESSAGES
Dreaming of escape from a tiger is generally seen as a good omen, and may herald the arrival of positive news.

NEGATIVE IMPLICATIONS
Being chased or caught by a tiger in a dream can forecast danger.

EMOTIONS
The tiger is generally seen as a symbol of fear, but it may also represent the cunning or manipulative side of your personality.

Positive messages

Lion dreams can relate to your actual or potential leadership skills. They can also reflect your power (real or imagined), and signify boldness, courage, and the ability to stand up with pride for yourself and your beliefs.

Negative implications

Fear of a dream lion can express worry about criticism from an authority figure. If the lion attacks you or seems about to pounce, it can mean that you feel you are under imminent threat.

LION

The lion has many mythical and contemporary connotations. It is the king of the jungle, the emblem of power, and a sign of the zodiac. It is also the cowardly creature in the film The Wizard of Oz, *seeking the strength to vanquish its timidity. Dreams about lions are most commonly linked to notions of bravery, pride, leadership, and protective rage. The dream lion may thus represent any of these aspects of the dreamer's personality or character.*

The context in which the dream lion appeared can have important ramifications for the dream's interpretation. The animal's appearance and how it behaved toward the dreamer are also relevant to

Head and ears

Dreaming of a lion's ears was traditionally thought to highlight fears that someone close to you is envious. The appearance of a lion's head in a dream can indicate that certain ambitions will be realized.

Roaring/playful lion

A lion roaring in an aggressive way suggests a need to deal with the jealousy of a friend or a deceit at work. A playful lion cub, on the other hand, can predict new and satisfying friendships.

Lion pride

A dream featuring a pride of lions indicates the possible start of a project in which you will lead or work closely with a team.

EMOTIONS

As head of the animal kingdom, the lion represents feelings of being in control. Riding on a lion's back may signify that you need protection or support from those who hold power over you.

the dream's interpretation. If the lion had some form of power over the dreamer, the ability to resist its fortitude can have implications for the dreamer's level of physical or psychological strength in waking life.

Fighting

A fight with a dream lion can be representative of a real dispute that has taken place in your waking life. Consider whether you were victorious in the dream or whether the dream lion defeated you. If you won, try to remember whether you were able to soothe the lion by calm actions or words.

Lioness

A dream lioness is generally seen as a sign of hope, particularly if she is seen protecting or lying down with her cubs. A lioness with her cubs may also symbolize positive familial relationships.

Sleeping lion

A sleeping lion can be interpreted as a sign that all is satisfactory within your "kingdom." Several lions sleeping may suggest that you should share your emotional contentment with others.

POSITIVE MESSAGES

Dog dreams are generally seen as good omens that center on friendship and commitment. They may relate to friendship in general, or be person-specific.

NEGATIVE IMPLICATIONS

Aggressive dogs usually indicate a fear of attack. Are you facing an aggressive colleague, or the unwelcome envy of someone in your social circle?

EMOTIONS

Your dream dog may represent someone you know. If so, the dream could refer to your present feelings toward that person. Is your relationship with the dog one of master and servant, or one of harmonious understanding?

DOG

As in the case of cat dreams, the dreamer's waking relationship with dogs has implications for the interpretation of his or her dreams which feature these animals. If the dreamer is afraid of dogs in waking life, a fearful dream involving a dog may be a simple reflection of this attitude. If the dreamer likes dogs but finds the dream dog frightening, however, this may reveal feelings of vulnerability within the dreamer, and the need to reevaluate his or her present situation.

Some analysts believe that dogs in dreams express "doglike" personality traits in the dreamer such as devotion, loyalty, and friendship. A dream dog may also represent a friend or acquaintance from the dreamer's waking life.

Barking dog

A dream dog barking with excitement or delight can express the feeling that you are socially accepted. A fiercely barking dog, however, may warn of potential work-related challenges ahead.

Fighting dogs

Dogs fighting in a dream may symbolize a battle between friends or family that you might be called upon to arbitrate. Was the fight short-lived? Who was the victor?

Big or small dog

A large dog could be a symbol of protection, referring to a soul-mate or loyal friend. A small dog suggests concerns that your friendships are insignificant.

POSITIVE MESSAGES

To attack or defeat a wolf can mean that several obstacles will be overcome in achieving a present goal. Where the wolf is part of a pack, this may indicate loyalty to one's family, friends, or colleagues.

NEGATIVE IMPLICATIONS

Some interpret the wolf as a symbol of cruelty, harshness, or disloyalty. To be bitten by a dream wolf can suggest that harm may come from your adversaries.

EMOTIONS

Wolves can denote fears of the "animal" within you, and of your potential to be destructive. Wolf dreams (especially those featuring aggressive wolves) are often associated with repression—usually of a sexual nature.

WOLF

The wolf has a deceptive, manipulative, and potentially cruel image. A dream about a wolf can symbolize those negative aspects of the dreamer's personality. Alternatively, as wolves in dreams are usually frightening, they may represent someone who the dreamer fears in his or her waking life.

It is important to note the nature of the wolf that appeared in the dream. For example, if the dream wolf was vulnerable, it could mean that the dreamer is making false assumptions about him- or herself, or about the personalities of close friends or relatives. Wolves can also carry sexual connotations; thus, a dream wolf may be linked to the dreamer's feelings about sex.

Pack of wolves/Wolf's head

The sight of many wolves running together in a menacing pack signifies a fear of being robbed or cheated. The sight of a wolf's head, however, can foretell success in the workplace.

Wolf's fangs/Howling wolf

The teeth of a wolf can symbolize fears of the unknown or anxiety about the future. A howling wolf may signal a "cry for help" from a family member or a close friend.

Fairytale wolf

The classic fairytale wolf, as depicted in *LITTLE RED RIDING HOOD*, may foretell a deception, warning that vigilance is needed. In a woman's dream, a fairytale wolf can symbolize a fear of male sexuality.

Dreaming in PURPLE

The color purple traditionally symbolizes authority, majesty, and the law. In Western societies, the legal professions and the monarchy are typically adorned in shades of purple. The appearance of purple in a dream, therefore, is said to represent loyalty, truth, justice, and spiritual penitence. Some claim that the color purple also expresses the dreamer's current state of psychic awareness, and can predict future happenings. The quality of the color can reflect the current state of the dreamer's mind, and may have implications for the dream's interpretation. The following dream animal symbols often appear in conjunction with the color purple, and can be interpreted as follows:

BIRD
A purple bird can be a symbol of pride, prowess, or personal dignity.

FISH
Exotic purple fish swimming together in a dream can signify free-flowing spirituality.

LEOPARD/CHEETAH
A purple leopard or cheetah may represent the strength of your emotions.

CAMEL
A dream about a purple camel can signify excessive subservience to an authority figure.

Other dream symbols commonly linked to the color purple include:

Procession
A purple procession can foretell the advent of pomp and ceremony in your future.

Crystal
Purple crystal may symbolize an unsolved mystery in your current waking life.

Glass
A purple glass can represent your intuition or self-awareness.

Flame
A purple flame can be a direct connection to your unconscious.

People
People tinted purple in a dream can foretell festive social occasions in your future.

Pen
A purple pen may signify that you need to be more truthful in your communications.

Book
A purple book can suggest that you lack self-confidence.

ACTIONS AND SITUATIONS

*A*lthough dreams about actions and situations tend to relate to personal experiences, they often occur in unfamiliar surroundings. The dreamer's emotional reaction to the action or situation can reflect his or her feelings toward waking life relationships and the direction his or her life is currently taking.

SHOPPING

The act of shopping is frequently connected to some form of gratification. Shopping dreams, therefore, are important indicators of the dreamer's needs and desires. Extravagant buying indicates a quest for immediate satisfaction, while a small purchase suggests a carefully reasoned approach to issues in the dreamer's life.

POSITIVE MESSAGES
Shopping dreams are tied to notions of freedom, choice, and the ability to make unhindered decisions.

NEGATIVE IMPLICATIONS
Hurried shopping can indicate a lack of self-restraint, especially in financial matters.

EMOTIONS
Dreams of shopping can directly reflect your current emotional needs. Were you calmly doing the week's shopping, or were you stocking up in case of an emergency?

Food
Food shopping in a dream can express a hidden attempt to "buy" other people's attention or devotion.

Desirable items
To dream of shopping for items you want may highlight the reality that you can't always get what you desire.

Store owner
A dream of owning or managing a store suggests feelings that people are too reliant on you.

GARDENING

The dream garden can be seen as a representation of the dreamer him- or herself, especially if the area tended was well-defined. Cultivation of a lush green garden can symbolize internal growth, and may suggest that the dreamer is in a positive phase of his or her life. Tending overgrown property implies that the dreamer is neglecting him- or herself or others.

POSITIVE MESSAGES
Dreams involving gardens can signify future gain and financial success.

NEGATIVE IMPLICATIONS
Gardening in a dream may signify sadness.

EMOTIONS
The garden's condition may reflect the current state of your psyche. Was it blooming or choked with weeds? Were the paths smooth or broken?

Seeds
The planting of seeds can symbolize the birth of new ideas.

Pruning
Pruning roses or other plants may symbolize tension in personal relationships.

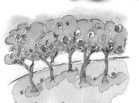

Orchard
An orchard in your dream can suggest that you are harvesting the fruits of your accumulated wisdom.

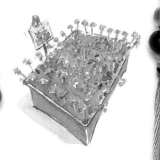

POSITIVE MESSAGES
Chasing someone or something denotes that you are working hard and expect to be rewarded for your efforts.

NEGATIVE IMPLICATIONS
Being chased is sometimes associated with a missed deadline, unfinished work, or some sort of threat.

EMOTIONS
Some believe that dreams of chases represent uncertainty, or anxiety about facing up to a situation that the dreamer would rather avoid. Consider the resolution of the dream chase. If you were the chaser, did you catch your quarry? If you were the hunted, were you captured?

CHASING OR BEING CHASED

Dreamed chases can be extremely vivid, whether the dreamer is the pursuer or the prey. A dream of being chased is likely to represent fear—of something in the real world, or, more often, in the unconscious. A dream in which the dreamer is the pursuer suggests that his or her conscious mind is "chasing" a part of his or her psyche which he or she fears. Answers to questions such as who or what was being chased, was the quarry caught, and what happened when the chase ended can help uncover the meaning of the dream.

Single pursuer
Being chased by one person in a dream is said to indicate a fear of intimacy in relationships.

Many pursuers
Being chased by a group may signify fears of being overwhelmed by work colleagues or family members, or of not having a say in some vital matter.

Unseen prey
Chasing unseen prey in a dream reveals directionless movement, and may suggest the need to clarify personal goals.

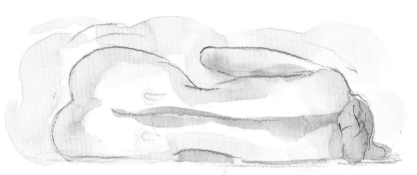

EMOTIONS

Dreams featuring nudity generally signify the desire to get beyond superficiality in personal relationships. Such dreams tell of yearnings to discover the "naked truth" about what makes a person tick.

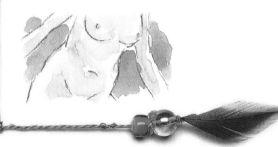

POSITIVE MESSAGES

Being naked in a dream can indicate that good luck or financial fortune may soon be coming your way.

NEGATIVE IMPLICATIONS

Nakedness in a dream can express a longing for childhood innocence, and for an escape from expectations of the adult world.

NAKEDNESS

A naked dream figure (the dreamer or another) can represent a yearning to reach back to the origin of life—in a general or a personal sense. Naked images are associated with life's beginnings and the innocence of early childhood. The biblical story of Adam and Eve describes their unashamed joy before they obtained knowledge and saw the world's complexities. Their story is echoed in the personal desire to return to an infant past untarnished by the realities of the adult world.

If the dreamer was naked in the dream and felt comfortable without any clothes on, this can imply a sense of comfort in his or her "own skin" in waking life.

Embarrassment

Shame at being naked in a dream can express a fear of being exposed or humiliated.

Exhibitionism

If you were flaunting your nudity in the dream, this may highlight a desire for new sexual encounters.

Nudity in others

Dreaming of others naked can imply that members of your inner circle are deceiving you in some way.

exams

Exams are hurdles that must be overcome in order to reach a new stage. Accordingly, success or failure in a dream exam can reflect the dreamer's inner thoughts about whether a problem can be resolved. Recurring exam dreams are common, and may represent judgments about passing or failing at different stages of life.

POSITIVE MESSAGES

Dreams of passing an exam with ease may foretell positive achievements and the realization of your goals.

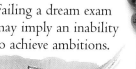

NEGATIVE IMPLICATIONS

Failing a dream exam may imply an inability to achieve ambitions.

EMOTIONS

Exam dreams are typically linked to anxieties about being unprepared, and to feelings of being tested in some way. Repeated exam dreams suggest feelings of failure.

Success

If you received a diploma for passing the exam, this reveals your ambition and pride in what you do.

Leaving early

Leaving an exam early may indicate arrogance or vanity. Ask yourself if you displayed such behavior recently in your waking life.

Cheating

Cheating on an exam can signify a sense of having attained something dishonestly.

SURGERY

The occurrence of surgery in a dream is usually thought to foretell change. Such dreams are often frightening, but they can also contain motivational messages. More literally, a dream of surgery may signal the need to repair an area of the dreamer's waking life.

POSITIVE MESSAGES

Operations in dreams can be harbingers of success or good news.

NEGATIVE IMPLICATIONS

Surgery dreams can reflect the need to overcome an obstacle.

EMOTIONS

Dreaming of surgery indicates that you are considering changes in your life; the operation is a metaphor for the spiritual or emotional repair work that you need to do.

Heart surgery

A dream of heart surgery indicates that your emotions need your attention.

Throat surgery

A throat operation may be connected to the need for improved channels of communication.

Neck surgery

Operations involving the neck are linked with themes of flexibility and the need to be adaptable in relationships and work matters.

SEX

Sex is a prevalent image in dreams and dream mythology. Many interpreters believe that sexual symbols represent the union between a person's male and female energies. A dream of a sexual act may reflect the joining of the complementary but contrasting sides of the self, signifying the integration of the dreamer's conscious and unconscious.

POSITIVE MESSAGES
Sexual dreams are often simple reflections of sexual desire or of past positive sexual encounters.

NEGATIVE IMPLICATIONS
Dreams that portray uninhibited sex may indicate that your real sex life is somehow stifled.

EMOTIONS
Sexual dreams are often about positive unions and the integration of connecting energies, and may provide an insight into your true sexual self.

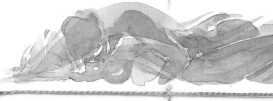

Teasing
Dreams about sexual teasing symbolize unfulfilled ambitions.

Unusual locations
Dreams of having sex in an unusual location can reflect a sense of exhibitionism or openness in you.

Unfamiliar practices
Participation in hitherto unexperienced sexual acts suggests a possible desire for experimentation in your waking life.

WASHING/BATHING

Washing and bathing carry connotations of cleansing, often in a spiritual sense. A dream that involves these activities may symbolize the disposal of old or unwanted feelings or attitudes. If the water the dreamer bathed in was dirty, this can imply that he or she is currently in the process of spiritual or emotional cleansing.

POSITIVE MESSAGES
Dreams of washing in a fountain or pool of clear water may signify personal happiness.

NEGATIVE IMPLICATIONS
Bathing with clothes on can be seen as a portent of imminent threat.

EMOTIONS
Washing and bathing dreams are often linked to the theme of "inner cleansing." They are seen as representations of the desire to create purity in life, whether in business, social, or family activities.

Face
Washing the face in a dream is sometimes linked to the ending of a dispute or long-standing argument.

Hair
Cleansing the hair denotes the ability to avoid potential danger.

Feet
Washing the feet can be seen as symbolic of unhappiness or dissatisfaction.

POSITIVE MESSAGES

Climbing dreams can be symbolic of your current prosperity, achievement, and sense of personal fulfillment.

NEGATIVE IMPLICATIONS

Climbing without ever reaching your destination shows a fear of failure in achieving a particular task or in completing a project.

CLIMBING

Dreams about climbing have many interpretations. Climbing is often associated with struggle—and with ultimate success if the dreamer reaches the summit. Climbing a mountain in particular can be seen as escapism, indulging a wish to run away from part or all of the dreamer's current life. The level of difficulty or ease with which the dreamer climbed may be a reflection of his or her progress in life, and how he or she tackles daily encounters. The dreamer's view from the top—and what he or she saw along the way—could shed light on waking dilemmas. If the view from the top was somehow obscured, however, this could have implications for the dreamer's approach to personal

Ladder

Ascending a ladder signifies honor and respect. Such an action is also associated with traditional stories, such as that of *JACOB'S LADDER*. Or, the ladder may represent a connection between different aspects of the self.

Tree

Climbing a tree implies ascending to a position of authority. Consider how quickly or slowly you were climbing, and how you felt if and when you eventually reached the top.

Wall

Scaling a wall denotes the need to find a solution—or some "sure footing"—with regard to a problem that may not yet be consciously recognized.

EMOTIONS

Consider how you felt during the climb. Were you anxious to get to the top, or were you calm, knowing it would happen eventually? Your emotions may be expressions of how you feel about your general progress in your waking life.

problems. Dreams of flying in an airplane and attempting to climb in altitude can represent the dreamer's awareness of the hurdles that he or she needs to overcome in waking life.

Airplane climbing over water

A dream of flying in an airplane climbing in altitude over a large expanse of water may represent the idea that you have taken on more than you can handle. Perhaps you have overestimated your ability to complete a certain project in your waking life.

Abyss below

The existence of an abyss below you if you fall from your climb may mean that you are currently undergoing a period of uncertainty or concern in your waking life. Such a dream may also refer to some form of personal journey that you are currently engaged in; the implication is that the journey is not over yet.

Low altitude

A dream airplane flying at a low altitude and attempting to climb back up is often connected to setbacks or difficulties within the dreamer's love life.

Dreaming in YELLOW

According to some dream analysts, the color yellow represents the dreamer's intellect and degree of linear thought. The appearance of yellow in a dream, therefore, may be a sign that the dreamer is thinking clearly and decisively in some sphere of his or her life. Yellow is also traditionally associated with fear and cowardice—hence the term "yellow streak." In the context of dream actions and situations, the symbols listed below often appear in conjunction with the color yellow, and can be interpreted as follows:

SHOOTING ARROWS
A dream of shooting yellow arrows or darts may indicate that you will reach your current goals by thinking clearly.

PLAYING BALL
If a yellow ball appears in a dream game, try to recall whether you contributed to the game—or whether you stood on the sidelines, too afraid to participate.

PLAYING IN A PLAYGROUND
Playing in a dream playground of a yellow hue may be evocative of feelings of exclusion in your younger days.

SITTING IN A ROOM
Sitting in a yellow room may be a sign of heightened awareness of a particular situation. Try to determine what that situation is, and whether there is anything you can do to improve it—for yourself or for those around you.

Other dream symbols commonly linked to the color yellow include:

Egg yolk
An egg yolk signifies notions of creativity and vitality.

Sun
A burning yellow sun can symbolize energy, strength, and the circle of life.

Food
Dreams about yellow foods, such as pasta or custard, can represent feelings of cowardice.

Bird
Yellow birds can reveal a yearning for liberation, or for an escape to a higher plane of existence.

Banana
A yellow dream banana can signal that you need an energy boost.

Flowers
Yellow flowers can symbolize creativity and change in your life.

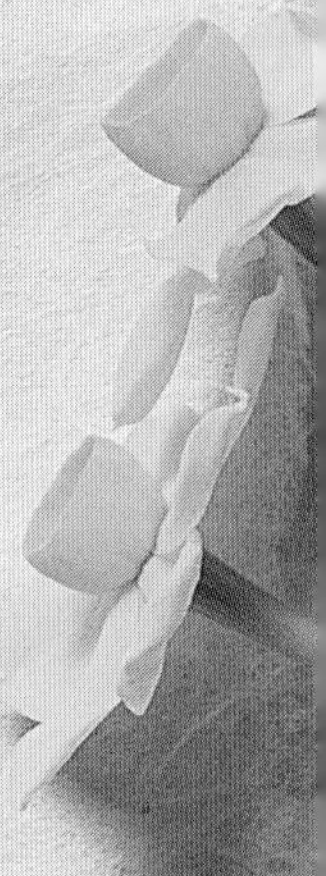

Notice
A yellow notice can be a sign that change will occur, but that setbacks may interrupt its pace.

Murky yellow
Murky yellow in a dream can reflect fears of sickness or failing health.

Grass
Yellow grass can be a signal that you are in need of physical or emotional nourishment.

EVERYDAY ITEMS

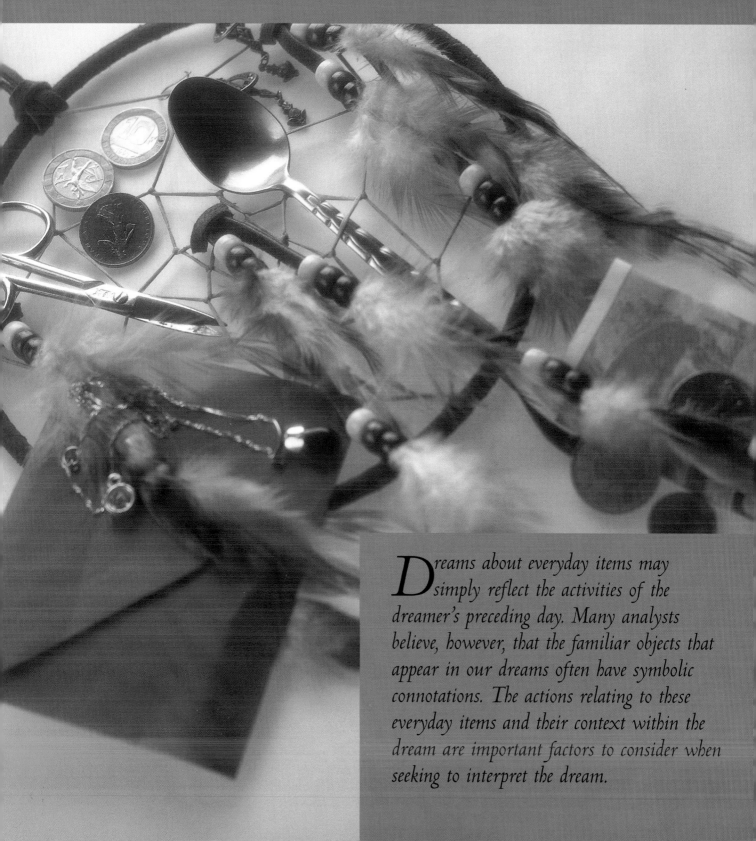

*D*reams about everyday items may simply reflect the activities of the dreamer's preceding day. Many analysts believe, however, that the familiar objects that appear in our dreams often have symbolic connotations. The actions relating to these everyday items and their context within the dream are important factors to consider when seeking to interpret the dream.

POSITIVE MESSAGES

A dream that focuses on leverage is generally interpreted as a wish for increased personal growth. Was the levering process difficult? If there was a problem, how was it ultimately overcome?

NEGATIVE IMPLICATIONS

Dreams featuring a plow can be tied to the need to resolve some form of emotional problem, and may indicate that strong, steady actions are needed to eradicate it.

EMOTIONS

Certain tools are thought to have sexual interpretations: A hammer driving in a nail has been linked to sexual intercourse, while a dream needle and thread are thought to symbolize early sexual experiences.

TⴲⴲLS

Dreams that feature tools are sometimes—but not always—interpreted as symbols of masculinity and male sexuality. The phallic form of certain tools obviously lends itself to this analysis. With their potential for digging and hiding, tools are also thought to represent elements that are locked away in the back of the dreamer's memory. It is important to recall how the tool was used in the dream, as this may have some bearing on the dreamer's psychological state. For example, if the tool was sweeping or clearing away debris in the dream, as opposed to simply shifting it from one place to another, this can imply a spiritual or psychological cleansing or rejuvenation.

Corkscrew

Dreams that feature corkscrews can relate to the "uncorking" of an idea or project. If the corkscrew worked with ease, a project may come to fruition with less effort than expected; if it was difficult to manipulate, obstacles may lie ahead.

Spade

As in waking life, dream spades can be used for digging and covering things over. If you were digging, were you searching for something—and if so, what? If an object was being concealed, was it associated with something that you may be unconsciously trying to avoid?

Level

A dream level may symbolize an attempt to keep things on an even keel—possibly in contrast to a past occasion, when a situation got out of control.

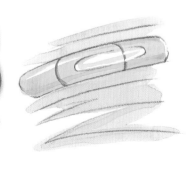

POSITIVE MESSAGES

Receiving dream money is generally considered a very good sign, especially if it was acquired through honest work or hard labor. Such dreams can also symbolize the flexing of your creative muscles.

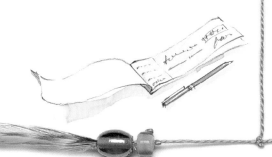

NEGATIVE IMPLICATIONS

Changing paper money for coins in the dream can denote problems in your financial strategy. Have you deferred an important monetary decision that will affect your future security?

EMOTIONS

Spending money freely in a dream can indicate feelings of goodwill and personal satisfaction. If you were window-shopping and unable to make a purchase, however, it may mean that you are feeling emotionally unfulfilled, or somehow deprived.

MONEY

Most interpreters believe that money dreams express the ability to give and receive in emotional terms. More literally, the dream may simply reflect the dreamer's waking use of money. Money can also signify the dreamer's generosity or greed. Thus, large amounts of dream money may indicate a magnanimous person—or the dreamer's desire to be one—whereas meager sums may suggest the dreamer's unwillingness (or inability) to part with generous amounts. Dream emotions on finding or seeing money can be significant as well. Surprise or joy can indicate prosperity ahead, whereas a knowing acceptance can reveal a current sense of financial satisfaction.

Borrowing money

Borrowing money in a dream may act as a warning not to indulge in an extravagant venture. Research all angles of a deal before you commit to a substantial personal undertaking.

Making payments

Giving money away in a dream is generally seen as a good sign relating to matters at work. Recall who was paid, how much, and why. The answers might shed light on current work-related issues.

Saving or investing

A dream of saving or investing money can be a straightforward reflection of financial planning for your future and that of your family. Or, it may imply that you have taken the necessary steps to emotionally prepare yourself for certain relationships.

POSITIVE MESSAGES

Receiving jewelry as a present can reveal the dreamer's sense of being recognized in some way. Who was the gift from—and why was it given? Was the present expected, or was it a surprise?

NEGATIVE IMPLICATIONS

A dream of viewing a rare jewel that you do not own can mean that you will fail to understand the importance of a particular future friendship. Failure to accept this friendship may cause difficulties later in life.

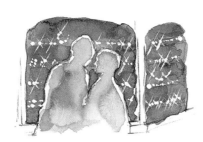

EMOTIONS

The loss of jewelry in a dream can reflect fears of loss in your waking life. You may be worried about losing a friendship or some valuable personal object.

JEWELRY

Dreams about jewelry are often connected with wish fulfillment. Jewels are adornments of the human form, and are used on special occasions. Dream jewels, therefore, can be linked to wishes pertaining to important events in the dreamer's life. There may even be a direct connection between the dream event where the jewels were worn and a real event in the dreamer's past or future. Sometimes, the dream jewels are viewed from a distance—possibly with envy or desire. Such dreams can represent the dreamer's aspiration for social standing, status, or monetary wealth. Alternatively, they can reflect the dreamer's envy of others on an emotional or psychological level.

Diamonds

Dreams about diamonds are often linked to personal relationships. The gem's many facets can imply the need to consider a relationship problem from a number of angles—or to examine the individual parts of the relationship rather than considering it as a whole.

Pearls

A dream of pearls around a woman's neck is generally seen as a positive sign, and can signify marriage or the possibility of children. The appearance of pearls in a dream may also relate to future transactions or purchases.

Rings

Dreams involving rings are often linked to the dreamer's sexuality. The dream ring may imply that your sexual nature is not entirely fulfilled at present, and that you should explore this aspect of yourself more fully. A dream ring can also symbolize the potential to become more committed to a relationship.

BROOM

Dreams of brooms typically represent the dreamer's desire to be rid of the past, or of current unwanted obligations. Or, they can be a cue for the dreamer that it is time to sweep out the "old clutter" in his or her life and begin new projects, relationships, or career choices.

POSITIVE MESSAGES
New brooms in dreams traditionally foretell good luck. They may signify the perception that good times lie ahead, and that chances should be seized.

NEGATIVE IMPLICATIONS
A damaged dream broom can reveal feelings of insecurity or suspicion of an acquaintance.

EMOTIONS
Reflect on where your dream broom was sweeping. What associations does that place have for you? Was the sweeping completed—or was it left unfinished?

Chasing with a broom
A dream of chasing someone with your dream broom could signify that a surprising change for the better is on the horizon.

Broom without bristles
If your dream broom had no bristles, this could mean that you are struggling to launch a new venture.

Yard broom
A dream broom that is stored or used outdoors may signify that you should consider or act upon matters not directly related to you occurring in the outside world.

GARBAGE

Dreams about garbage can signal that the dreamer is trying to jettison unwanted aspects of his or her life. The substance of the waste material and what it might represent can be significant to the dream's interpretation.

POSITIVE MESSAGES
Dreams concerning garbage disposal can be perceived as an attempt to rid your life of any wasteful elements, and to focus on the positive.

NEGATIVE IMPLICATIONS
A dream that others were disposing of your garbage might indicate a concern that others are carrying your burdens for you.

EMOTIONS
Was the garbage dumped close to you, or transported far away? How did you feel after it was disposed of?

Covered in garbage
A dream in which you were covered in garbage can imply feelings of being overburdened in your waking life. Note if and how you escaped—did someone help you, or did you manage alone?

Discovery in the garbage
A valuable object in your dream garbage may foretell an unexpected piece of good news in the near future.

Valuables thrown away
If precious goods were unwittingly placed in the garbage, try to figure out who put them there. Is there someone close to you who may be trying to spoil an event or project?

SCISSORS

Dreams of scissors can be associated with the cutting out of aspects of the dreamer's emotional, personal, or active waking life. It is important to note what exactly was being cut in the dream, how precise the incisions were, and who was actually doing the cutting.

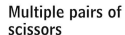

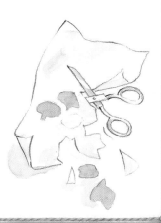

POSITIVE MESSAGES

An unused pair of dream scissors can foretell that you will soon enter a romantic relationship. If you are already involved, the dream may reflect a desire to make this bond more permanent.

Multiple pairs of scissors

A dream featuring multiple pairs of scissors may represent feelings of unrequited love. Perhaps you should "cut" your links with a love interest who is not reciprocating your feelings.

NEGATIVE IMPLICATIONS

The appearance of scissors in your dream may warn that you are dividing your attention between projects or ambitions—and may thus fail to realize any of your goals.

Scissors cutting

Using scissors to cut in your dream can reflect the perception that you will outwit a rival in work or personal matters.

EMOTIONS

If you were cutting in the dream, the scissors may represent an extension of your personality. Were you making decisive incisions? Or were you struggling to separate the cut pieces?

Indecisiveness

Dreams of scissors can sometimes represent feelings of indecisiveness. Such dreams may forecast the importance of making a decision that you had been procrastinating.

ENVELOPE

The meaning of dreams featuring envelopes can depend on the context of the envelope in the dream and the dreamer's emotional response to it. That said, a dream envelope often symbolizes a message that the dreamer wishes to communicate— or one which he or she is anticipating. The contents of the envelope and whether it was sealed can be important factors in the dream's interpretation.

POSITIVE MESSAGES

Dreams of open envelopes may represent the onset of trivial problems that can easily be overcome.

Many envelopes

A dream of many envelopes can suggest the expectation of news, or that new projects are on the horizon. Note how you felt upon opening the envelopes. Did they hold any messages for you?

NEGATIVE IMPLICATIONS

A tightly sealed dream envelope can signal difficult emotional or practical obstacles. Look to your dream for clues to over-coming these hurdles.

Sealed packet of envelopes

A sealed packet of envelopes can signify the anticipation of a change of direction in life. Such a dream may, however, suggest uncertainty about the best way to achieve these changes.

EMOTIONS

An inability to open an envelope in a dream may symbolize frustration at being unable to find a solution to a problem.

Packed envelope

If the dream envelope is filled to bursting, it can indicate that you are feeling overwhelmed by work matters or by a relationship.

POSITIVE MESSAGES

A dream about food can be viewed as a positive sign, especially if you ate and were satisfied. A hearty meal or delicious snack consumed with pleasure can reveal a deep sense of satisfaction with your life. It can also indicate a belief that good times are ahead, or that groundwork is in place that will lead to future benefits.

NEGATIVE IMPLICATIONS

Eating or drinking in a gluttonous manner can express the "ravenous" side of your nature, reflecting needs that are currently unfulfilled, and perhaps compensating for feelings of being unsupported or unloved. Such dreams can also highlight the fear that present good times may be short-lived, and must be enjoyed while they last.

FOOD & DRINK

Food and drink are a significant part of our waking lives, so it is not surprising that they often appear in our dreams. Items of food and drink frequently represent affection, appetite, or a desire to live life to the fullest. Some analysts believe that biting or chewing in a dream is connected with sensual pleasures. Dreams of overeating can point to an emotional or practical overload in the dreamer's life. Conversely, meager amounts of food or drink can be a sign that the dreamer is currently feeling deprived and needs some form of "nourishment." Consider the type of food or drink in the dream—was it familiar or strange? Comfort foods from childhood times, for example,

Rich foods

Dreams of rich foods, such as creamy sauces and chocolate, are said to be signs of extravagance. Note how you felt while consuming the food. Did you feel guilty about the quality or the abundance of it, or did you feel justified in enjoying it?

Wine

Wine is traditionally associated with pleasure and ritual—the celebration of weddings and births, for example. If the dream wine was consumed in company, you may be planning a joyous event, even if the occasion has not yet been officially acknowledged.

Breakfast foods

Just as breakfast is the first meal of the day, the dream breakfast—or breakfast items such as cereals and toast—can mark the beginning of a new project, or a new stage in your life. Was the breakfast consumed at a leisurely pace, or was it rushed?

EMOTIONS

The quality of your dream food and drink, and your feelings toward them, are significant to the interpretation of your dream. For example, a dream of eating leftovers may show that you are living on the "bare minimum." Think about the quality and quantity of life's ingredients that you need to enrich your waking life, and how these can be obtained.

may represent a yearning to return to less troubled times. The context in which the dreamer was eating or drinking—at a social occasion, for example—can reflect those aspects of the dreamer's life which are in need of attention or some form of nourishment.

Eggs

A dream featuring eggs may relate to the circle of life itself. Eggs also symbolize fertility and growth, so dream eggs can represent the evolution of new ventures—or the development of new aspects of yourself, either consciously or unconsciously. If the eggshell is broken, a situation or emotion may need to "break through" to your conscious mind so that you can deal with it.

Dairy products

Dreams about dairy products can be inner yearnings for things past. Symbolic of the nurturing bond between mother and child, milk in a dream can reflect dependency or a desire for an emotional "feeding" from someone close to you.

Restaurant

The atmosphere of your dream restaurant can reveal your emotional state. Wholesome or elegant surroundings indicate contentment with life, while a dimly lit establishment, where the service is poor and the food mediocre, may indicate a need for inspiration or some form of personal satisfaction currently missing from your life.

POSITIVE MESSAGES

Dreams of spoons can symbolize enduring domestic or familial happiness. Spoons that scoop up food can represent nourishment, and may signify that life is good and you are "enjoying your fill."

NEGATIVE IMPLICATIONS

Some say a knife appearing in a dream is a bad omen, and can imply that current pleasures are about to be "cut" in some way. To dream of giving a knife as a present can denote the premature severing of a project. Consider this dream a warning, and think about how you might circumvent such trouble in your waking life.

EMOTIONS

Think about the context in which the dream cutlery appeared. Who was using it? If you were struggling with any of the utensils—peas falling off your fork, for example, or your knife being unable to cut the food—it may be a sign that you are feeling frustrated, or are having trouble getting the nourishment you need.

CUTLERY

Many people believe that dreams involving cutlery represent the masculine and feminine aspects of the dreamer. Dreaming of a knife and fork together can also signify a balanced lifestyle. Any associations that the dream cutlery has in the dreamer's waking life is also significant. For example, if the dream featured old-fashioned cutlery, this might be connected with dreamer's grandparents or with childhood experiences. If the cutlery was modern and unfamiliar, it may signify the dreamer's desire to embark on new projects or a new phase of life. The appearance of cutlery in the context of eating can symbolize nourishment, and may thus signify healthy emotional or personal growth.

Shiny spoon

To dream of a shiny spoon can symbolize that your home life is running smoothly. Similarly, a set of new spoons can indicate harmony within the family group.

Fork

A dream fork that is used to blend tasty ingredients can foretell busy and enjoyable social events in the near future.

Knife

A dream knife that appears rusty or broken can reflect your fears concerning some form of family strife or love life problems. Was the knife left to deteriorate, or was it taken in for repairs?

POSITIVE MESSAGES

A dream container which holds its contents comfortably, without overcrowding, can be a sign that future obstacles will be overcome. Did you pack the dream container yourself? If so, you may already be planning how to deal with any problems that may arise.

NEGATIVE IMPLICATIONS

If your dream container was packed with personal effects, this could indicate a need to "get rid of the old and bring in the new." What significance do these items hold in your waking life? If they are important, you may need help in your "spring cleaning."

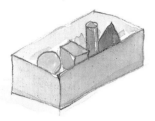

EMOTIONS

The interpretation of dream containers varies according to their form and appearance, how they were handled, and the presence of other people in the dream. Were the containers safely packed? If they were battered or leaking, this may signify a need for greater caution in your waking life.

CONTAINERS

Dreams of containers, such as boxes and bags, are generally said to represent areas of the dreamer's psyche. Such dreams can allude to notions of security, safety, and containment—in an emotional or a real sense. Alternatively, a dream featuring heavy containers could be a signal that the dreamer needs to unload some sort of burden. The contents of the dream containers, if any, can be significant to uncovering the dream's meaning. An empty dream container may signify that the dreamer's waking life needs filling, either emotionally or with new challenges. If the container held another person's possessions, this could be a sign of envy and the desire to pursue someone else's lifestyle.

Empty box

An empty box in your dream may be telling you that something is missing from your life. Did you open the box to discover that it was empty—and were you surprised to find it this way? Your reaction may reflect your present level of emotional satisfaction.

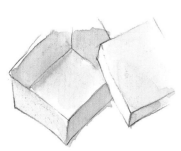

Pocketbook/Wallet

With its sections for the owner's most personal possessions, a dream pocketbook or wallet can be equated with the most private aspects of your emotional world. Was the dream pocketbook or wallet full or empty? Were you frightened of losing it?

Jar/Pot

Jars or pots can symbolize social gatherings, or a desire to expand your immediate circle of friends. Overflowing jars or pots may signify that you feel overwhelmed by emotional or personal issues.

Dreaming in PINK

Pink is usually associated with love—particularly unconditional love. Some also connect pink with the healing powers of the human soul or with the heart chakra (the center of psychic or spiritual energy). In the context of dreams, the everyday items listed below often appear in conjunction with the color pink, and can be interpreted as follows:

WINDOW

The image of a pink window can represent a personal opportunity that has not yet been revealed.

CLOTH/MAT

Dreams of a pink cloth or mat may mean that you are considering entering into a new relationship or friendship, and are weighing the implications of this new involvement.

CLOSET

A pink closet can signify that you are currently storing love for someone special while waiting for the right moment to reveal your feelings.

CLOTHES

Pink clothes can indicate a wish to be "covered" in love by someone close. You may be seeking attention or compassion.

CHAIR

A pink chair may signify emotional stability, especially if it remains unmoved during the dream.

Other dream symbols commonly linked to the color pink include:

Flowers

Pink flowers are usually interpreted as symbols of future pleasurable social activities.

Statue

A pink statue can be a sign of success in a work project.

Steps

Pink steps may suggest that you will accomplish a personal task through hard work.

Poster

A pink poster can indicate a potentially beneficial transaction in the near future.

Figure/Face

A pink figure or face may signify that you are in the process of revealing deep emotional feelings to someone in your waking life.

Heart

A pink heart or heart shape could be related to pangs of love for someone far away.

TRAVEL

*T*ravel in dreams does not necessarily reflect a real journey; it is more often associated with the dreamer's "journey" through life. Dream travel can also be interpreted as a wish to escape some aspect of life. Beginning a journey implies adventure, a counterbalance to the mundane elements of daily routine.

NEGATIVE IMPLICATIONS

A rough boating trip may mean that you are undergoing a period of emotional turmoil. Were there calm seas ahead?

EMOTIONS

The safety of a vessel carrying passengers across stormy seas can symbolize your home life, or present emotional well-being.

POSITIVE MESSAGES

Dreams of boats can portray optimism and an enjoyable future journey—real or emotional. They suggest easy movement and the realization of your goals.

B⊕aτ

Dreams about boats are often portrayed as life-affirming. Many interpreters see the boat as a symbol of optimism and a sign that promising developments are just over the horizon. Like other methods of transportation in dreams, boats are also sometimes said to represent periods of transition or change. The condition of the boat may represent the status of the dreamer's emotional life—the dreamer's relationship with his or her family, or a current love interest may be reflected.

It is relevant to consider the sailing conditions in the dream; a tranquil sea carries different meanings than choppy and dangerous waters. The pace and destination of the dream boat may reflect the speed at which the dreamer is achieving his or her ambitions.

Clear waters/Walking on a boat

Dreaming of boating on a river, lake, or clear-water pond can signify happiness and success in your waking life. Walking on a boat can foretell future harmony and contentment.

Drifting

A boat that is drifting points to the possibility of a deep-rooted fear of "drifting" in your personal life. It can also highlight worries that you are disorganized in business matters.

Capsizing

A boat that appears to be in danger of overturning can indicate a sense of present danger and the need to take evasive action.

POSITIVE MESSAGES

Carrying luggage in a dream can forecast a long trip or expedition. This could be a physical journey, a change of relationship, or a new work venture. Dreams of luggage can also represent excitement, and may follow the announcement of a new opportunity.

NEGATIVE IMPLICATIONS

Lost luggage usually reflects anxiety that things are getting out of hand. Heavy or cumbersome bags may symbolize a burden that you are currently shouldering. A dream in which you must constantly carry heavy baggage can suggest that a particular burden will be difficult to shed.

LUGGAGE

Luggage can be a powerful dream symbol. For many, dream luggage is directly linked to the burden of emotional stresses, and the need to shed them. Dream luggage can also represent unexplored personal issues that weigh on the dreamer's conscious or unconscious mind and emerge in the dream to encourage the search for resolution. In this way, dream luggage can be connected to a profound journey toward the discovery of the dreamer's true self.

The luggage carried in a dream can also symbolize the dreamer's emotional ties, and the weight of the bags can indicate how the dreamer really feels about family members or friendships. It is

Packing and unpacking

A dream of placing objects inside a bag can mean that you hope to stock up on the good things in life. Unpacking a bag may be a sign of positive steps toward freeing yourself from a problematic relationship or an unrewarding job.

Purse

A woman's dream of losing her change purse or some or all of its contents can symbolize a loss of personal belongings or of parts of her identity.

Trunk

A dream trunk can denote a long and profound voyage of self-discovery. You may be frightened of the trunk's contents, yet be tempted to open it. If you opened the dream trunk, consider whether its contents symbolize any worries in your waking life.

EMOTIONS

Luggage sometimes symbolizes elements in your life that should be disposed of. Some analysts say that luggage dreams represent your unconscious telling you it is time to pack your bags and move on. Recall the luggage in your dream. Were your dream bags lighter than you had anticipated?

important to note how the bags were transported: were they hand-held or carried on a vehicle? What did they contain—and what implications might these contents have for the dreamer in waking life? Some analysts believe that the appearance of luggage simply signifies that the dreamer is in need of a holiday.

Size of luggage

A very large piece of luggage may represent a heavy commitment or series of commitments that you are facing in your waking life. Did you know what the contents of your dream bags were? If so, could these contents have been re-packed in a number of smaller, more manageable bags?

Luggage for sale

The appearance of luggage in a store window may indicate a desire to change your job. If you purchased the luggage in the dream, this may mean that you are considering making a positive career move in the near future. Looking longingly at the dream luggage without purchasing it can indicate feelings of being held back from making a move.

Safety and security

Some analysts see luggage as representing the instinct for self-preservation or security. Your dream luggage may symbolize a womb, signifying a wish to return to a state where you were protected from the complications of the world.

POSITIVE MESSAGES

Straight roads signify smooth and continuous progress in life, and the prospect of trouble-free journeys ahead.

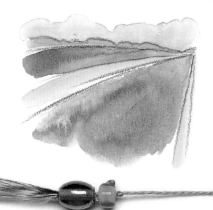

NEGATIVE IMPLICATIONS

Winding roads suggest difficulties in the near future, and a range of hazardous obstacles to tackle before your journey's end.

EMOTIONS

Dream roads are generally connected to the direction you feel your life is taking. If the destination in the dream was clear, you are probably certain where you are heading. If you fail to reach your destination, ask yourself what is preventing you from achieving your goals.

HIGHWAYS & ROADS

Dream highways and roads are thought to represent the "journey" of life. The length and quality of the road or highway can signify the present state of the dreamer's emotional "travel." A smooth road or highway can indicate inner peace, while a bumpy road or highway can symbolize emotional or spiritual disquiet. When a road or highway appears in a dream, it is important to note where it was headed. Any repetitive features along the route might represent a particular pattern in the dreamer's life. If there were signposts along the way, it may be important for the dreamer to heed their instructions in waking life.

City

Negotiating a complex layout of city streets may show that you are currently trying to solve complicated life dilemmas.

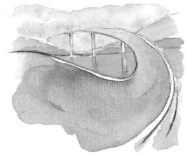

Freeway

Freeway driving portrays a speedy journey, and can indicate that you will soon achieve your goals.

Uphill

An uphill drive is sometimes thought to reflect a struggle— physical or emotional—that demands your attention.

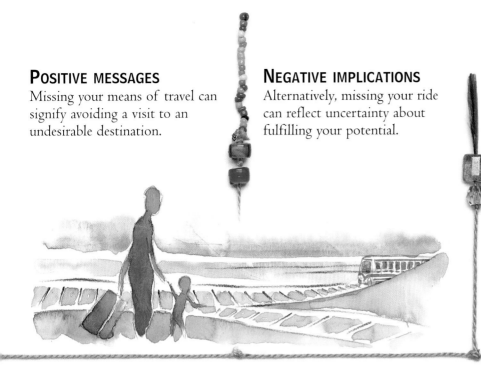

POSITIVE MESSAGES
Missing your means of travel can signify avoiding a visit to an undesirable destination.

NEGATIVE IMPLICATIONS
Alternatively, missing your ride can reflect uncertainty about fulfilling your potential.

EMOTIONS
Your dream of missed transportation may portray fears of missing a job opportunity or social engagement. Think about how you missed your ride. Was the vehicle still in sight, or had it departed long ago? The answer might relate to your distance from your goals.

MISSED TRANSPORTATION

Missing a means of transportation may simply reflect an actual fear of late arrival or the inability to meet a deadline. Some such dreams, however, can hold deeper meanings that relate to the dreamer's emotional strengths and weaknesses. The cause of the dreamer missing the means of transportation should be considered. If he or she was somehow impeded, the factor that presented the obstruction may represent a person or object that the dreamer feels is to blame for a waking life problem. If the lateness was the dreamer's fault, this may reflect anger over an action or omission in waking life.

Accidental delay
A physical mishap that delays you could symbolize something in your life that you seek to blame for a misfortune.

Careless delay
Carelessness in missing your means of transportation may show a need to become more organized, or reflect an unconscious desire not to embark on a certain journey.

Anger at delay
Anger at missing a scheduled departure may echo anger over an omission in your daily life.

BUS

The bus's travels in the dream can provide insight into how the dreamer is presently negotiating his or her life's journey. It is significant to note whether the bus was following a fixed route, or driving aimlessly to an unspecified location. The dreamer's role in relation to the bus—as passenger or driver—can reflect a sense of control over his or her own life or the lives of others.

POSITIVE MESSAGES
Bus travel in your dream can be a sign that you are well on your way to achieving your goals.

NEGATIVE IMPLICATIONS
Prolonged waiting at a bus stop symbolizes frustration on the path toward your ambitions.

EMOTIONS
Try to recall if the bus ride was bumpy. If it was, how did that make you feel?

Bus accident
A bus accident can reveal fears of impending financial difficulties.

Double-decker
If the dream bus is a "double-decker," this may imply that you should try looking at things on more than one level.

Driving a bus
Being the driver of your dream bus can show that you feel responsible for a group of people, such as friends or colleagues.

PASSENGER

If the dreamer is a passenger, the dream may relate to the extent to which he or she feels in control of his or her life at the moment. Carrying passengers in a vehicle can be connected to partnership or cooperation. Stopping to pick up a passenger may signify that the dreamer is opening his or her mind up to new possibilities.

POSITIVE MESSAGES
Passenger dreams suggest freedom from responsibilities while someone else shoulders the burden.

NEGATIVE IMPLICATIONS
Alternatively, being a passenger can mean that you feel out of control. Carrying passengers may express worries about others being a burden to you.

EMOTIONS
A group of passengers in your dream may represent aspects of your emotional self.

Passenger on wheels
Traveling as a passenger in a wheeled vehicle is generally seen as signifying success.

Rocket or balloon
Rocket or balloon travel can express the desire to escape from a current life situation.

In a crowd
Finding yourself among a crowded passenger group suggests you feel "hemmed in."

AIRPLANE

A dream airplane on its soaring flight path is consistently related to notions of escape and freedom. Flight can represent the "taking off" of a new proposal, or the potential to leap forward in a particular setting. The situation of the plane can be important: Was it cruising high above the clouds, or hovering near the ground?

POSITIVE MESSAGES
Piloting an airplane in a dream can represent an unexpected or unusual success in your life, perhaps in connection with work.

NEGATIVE IMPLICATIONS
Airplanes dropping bombs can be portents of bad news. A fleet of bombers indicates that trouble may lie ahead.

EMOTIONS
The symbolism of an airplane can mirror that of a bird: freedom and release.

Taking off
Taking off in a dream airplane may anticipate embarkation on a new project.

Landing
Coming in to land may reveal that you are close to finalizing a work arrangement or personal matter.

Circling
Circling in the air can portray a feeling of going nowhere. If you are in a negative cycle, consider how to break out of it.

TRAIN

Dream trains can symbolize security, elation, or postponement, depending on their movement. The dreamer's position in relation to the train—as a passenger, standing alongside it, or awaiting its arrival—can hold clues to the dream's meaning. Some analysts associate the image of a train entering a tunnel with the dreamer's deep-rooted sexual feelings.

POSITIVE MESSAGES
Dreams of moving trains can signify your sense of security about the direction your life is presently taking.

NEGATIVE IMPLICATION
A stationary train can indicate a hitch in your current plans.

EMOTIONS
Some analysts construe the train as the male sexual organ. Entering a tunnel therefore represents coitus. If your dream train was headed toward a tunnel, how did that make you feel?

Waiting for a train
Awaiting a dream train may simply represent the expectation of future success.

Sudden halt
If the dream train comes to an emergency stop, be wary of rushing ahead with new projects.

Grade crossing
Closed gates at a grade crossing can indicate that you need to bide your time.

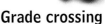

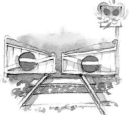

POSITIVE MESSAGES

Dreaming of an automobile journey can mean that you have the chance to make a comfortable living and to take charge of your working life.

NEGATIVE IMPLICATIONS

Automobile crashes are symbols of conflict, confusion, and lack of control in your present life. Consider what happened at the scene of the accident. Who was involved in the crash? Were you able to help the victim?

AUTOMOBILE

Many people dream of automobiles: their own, their friends', or completely unfamiliar vehicles. For some, the dream automobile is a representation of the self. If the dreamer was at the wheel, this may signify a sense of control over his or her life, and the feeling that a suitable life path is being taken. If the dreamer was a passenger, this may signify a general need for greater empowerment, or to be less reliant on others.

The smoothness of the ride is thought to reflect the dreamer's underlying emotions, while its velocity is believed to represent the speed at which the dreamer is achieving his or her goals in life.

Woman's dream

Women's dreams of cars are often said to represent ambitious feelings and their desire to "overtake" the significant men in their lives.

Man's dream

Most dream analysts associate men's car dreams with power, masculinity, and sexuality.

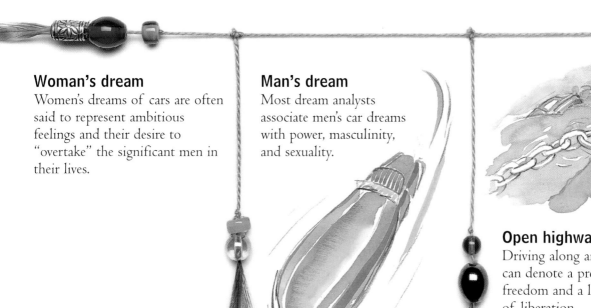

Open highway

Driving along an open highway can denote a present feeling of freedom and a lifetime journey of liberation.

EMOTIONS

Automobile dreams are often perceived as being related to the dreamer's "drive" in life. If you were a passenger, were you in the back or the front of the vehicle? How did you feel about where you were seated? What was your ultimate destination? How did you feel when you arrived?

Some commentators view the automobile as a symbol of the male sexual organ or of sexual powers in general.

Speeding car

A dream of riding in a car that is driving above a specified speed limit can signify the hope that your ability to pay attention to detail will help you succeed in life.

Backseat driver

A passenger in the backseat of your dream car who insists that you, the driver, follow a particular path, may indicate the existence of some force or person in your life attempting to push you in a direction that you do not wish to go. If you listened to the backseat driver, ask yourself whether someone or something is manipulating you in your waking life.

Car parts

Different car parts can be connected to various aspects of your waking personality. Headlights may be tied to the general direction in which your "life path" is taking you; the gas level may be connected to your energy levels; and steering a car might be tied to ideas of confidence, independence and self-control.

Dreaming in
⊕RANGE

Orange is commonly thought to symbolize nobility and generosity. It can also represent radiance, optimism, and tranquility. Dreams in which orange appears can therefore signify positive change in the dreamer's waking life. Some contend, however, that the color orange also suggests feelings of mistrust and doubt, and thus a dream in which it features may reveal discontent or uncertainty. The travel-related symbols below often appear in conjunction with the color orange, and can be interpreted as follows:

RUNNING SHOES
Orange running shoes can represent positive movement toward a future destination. Their appearance may be tied to a current project that is on the verge of completion.

PASSPORT
An orange passport could be a signal to proceed with an activity—the color implies a successful outcome.

MAP
An orange map or atlas may illustrate a desire to travel, or to seek out new terrain, either practically or emotionally.

EARTH
Orange soil denotes a positive journey— possibly in connection with work or work colleagues.

Other dream symbols commonly linked to the color orange include:

Orange blossom
A dream of an orange blossom may have been prompted by the arrival of troubling news.

Sour orange
Despite its unpleasant taste, a sour orange can be a sign of happiness.

Elevator
An orange elevator can denote an upturn in your emotional state following a depressed period.

Hat
An orange hat can symbolize creativity, or the dawning of a bright new idea.

Arm/Fist
An orange arm or fist can denote feelings of hostility or aggression.

Flower
An orange flower can represent feelings of vitality and a general contentment with your life.

Volcano
An orange volcano can express a surge of creativity that is waiting to burst through.

Orange you
If you appear orange in your dream, this can be a sign of self-protection or of self-love.

Highway sign
An orange highway sign can denote that an expected change in your current situation could be delayed.

making the most of your dreams

There are a number of ways to make studying and interpreting your dreams easier, and methods of encouraging dreaming as well. A dream diary is useful to help you remember your dreams, and can prompt you to notice any recurrent themes. A spiritual tool called a "dream catcher" is used by some Native American tribes, and in parts of Asia, to guard against bad dreams. Assorted oils, herbs, and relaxing remedies can help you relax and prepare for dreaming. There are also special techniques which can be used to influence the content of your dreams.

KEEPING a DREAM DIARY

Although we cannot always remember our dreams, they often leave us with feelings that remain with us during our waking hours. Recording our dreams can help us remember them, and can thus help identify the sources of these lingering emotions.

Writing it down

Most dream analysts recommend recording the contents of your dreams in a dream diary. In addition to helping you recall the dream's details, the diary will provide a record for study, enabling you to identify patterns and themes within your dreams.

A psychological and practical commitment to the process of recording your dreams is the first step on the path to interpretation.

Initial notes

There are no rules about the form that the diary should take—just choose a method that you find practical to maintain. Most people keep a notebook and a flashlight by their beds, but an audio diary would work just as well. Try to record your dream before getting out of bed, as activity can cause it to "disappear."

Initial dream notes should be relatively brief—an outline will do at this point. Be sure, however, that your notes mention even the seemingly trivial or obscure aspects of the dream, as these can contain clues to its meaning.

A full account

As soon as possible after making your initial notes, while the dream is still fresh in your mind, record it in full. A large diary or exercise book is recommended, with enough space to write down the details of the dream on the left-hand side—the recollection page—and any thoughts and associations on the right-hand side—the interpretation page. Some analysts suggest using diagrams and pictures to facilitate memories of images or events in the dream.

The recollection page

Always note the date of the dream, as this may be relevant to its meaning. For example, the dream might occur on a significant anniversary, or when a deadline is looming. Dated pages can also help to contextualize a dream if you are chronicling a series of dreams. Record the dream in the exact sequence in which it unfolded. Try to leave a space between different "scenes."

The interpretation page

Give your interpretation page headings such as positive messages, negative implications, and emotions. It is also useful to note whether any colors appeared, and if so, whether they were affiliated with specific objects or persons. You might base your notes on the Directory of Dream Symbols (pages 18-131). Use the categories from the Directory (life and death, forces of nature, and so on) as a basis for your analysis, adding your own as you see fit. Be sure to note any events from the previous day that may have influenced your dream. It can also be helpful to write down what you were thinking about just prior to falling asleep.

Recurring themes

Read back over the contents of your diary occasionally; you may notice recurring themes in your dreams. It can be useful to add an overall analysis page to your diary from time to time, in order to tie recent themes together.

PREPARING TO DREAM

If you hope to have dreams to analyze, it is important to get a good night's sleep. Anxieties from your waking hours can inhibit the process of sleeping and dreaming. The following methods of preparation for sleep and dreaming are based on documented research and on individual experience.

Sleep routines

It is important not to sleep during the day if you want a good night's sleep. However tired you are, try to stay awake, so that your mind and body are fully aware of the differences between the waking zone and the sleeping zone. For consistently good sleep, it is wise to go to bed at approximately the same time each night. During the day, try to make sure you get enough exercise, eat balanced meals, and do not drink too much coffee or other caffeinated beverages, such as tea and cola drinks. Avoid alcohol and cigarettes for a few hours before going to bed, as both can disturb your sleep pattern.

The sleep environment

Since we spend approximately one third of our lives sleeping, the environment in which we sleep should be well designed for the purpose. The room should be peaceful and uncluttered, preferably without a television or telephone. It should also be well aired, and neither too hot nor too cold; the recommended temperature is 65° F (18° C). If the atmosphere feels too dry or too stuffy, increase the humidity by placing bowls of water around the room, or damp towels over a radiator, or invest in an air humidifier.

Obviously, the most important item in your sleeping room is the bed. You should buy the best mattress you can afford. It must be firm enough to support your back without sagging, especially as the muscles lose tension during REM sleep, leaving the ligaments to take the strain.

Lighting is significant when preparing your body for sleep. The brighter the lighting, the harder it is for your body to achieve a state of relaxation. Make full use of dimmer switches, low-voltage lamps, and gently colored lampshades. Make sure that your drapes are thick enough to block out street lights or sunshine—they can be lined, if necessary, with light-resistant fabric.

Pillows should be soft and comfortable, but firm enough to support your neck. It does not matter if your pillows are filled with synthetic materials or feathers, but allergy sufferers should avoid feathers. The pillow should support your head rather than raise it.

Soothing scents

To gain the most from your dreams, it is important to prepare for sleep calmly. Sometimes the associations of a particular smell can induce feelings of comfort. Scented candles are popular for this purpose and are widely available. Or, relaxing aromatherapy oils such as lavender, cypress, rose, marjoram, and camomile can be added to a bath, vaporized, or massaged into the skin, using a carrier oil such as almond oil. Essential oils are carried by most health food stores and some drug stores as well, and are often

recommended for sleep disorders. It is important to use caution when choosing aromatherapy products, however—for example, some essential oils must not be used by pregnant women. Advice from a qualified aromatherapist is recommended.

Relaxation techniques

Relaxation is not a passive activity—it requires a combination of physical and mental techniques, and a determination to focus the entire body and mind.

Most people can, nevertheless, find a method of physical and mental relaxation that works for them. Many people find that taking a warm bath aids relaxation. This is usually most effective about a half-hour before bed. A warm milky drink, a camomile tea, or a herbal infusion at bedtime can also be helpful. Some people listen to calming music while preparing for bed.

Visualization (or imagery) is another popular method of relaxing for sleep. This process involves conjuring up images that will promote positive feelings in general—a peaceful, restful place, for example—and empty the mind of troubled, distressing, or overstimulating images. Because of its ability to reduce stress and aid in relaxation, visualization can be an effective aid to sleep.

Gentle muscle relaxation, deep breathing, meditation, or yoga exercises may help prepare you for sleep as well. These methods can require a little practice, but in

time they may become a beneficial aid—not just to help you sleep, but also for your general well-being. Be sure to switch off your phone, so that callers do not interfere with the process of relaxation.

If you have little success with sleep-inducing techniques, however, do not remain in bed tossing and turning. It is better to get up and spend some time away from the bedroom, relaxing or listening to music, before trying to get to sleep again.

Watching television, reading a stimulating book, or taking a walk as a means of distraction when you cannot sleep may not be helpful, as such activities activate the mind and body and can inhibit relaxation, and thus sleep.

Dream Catchers

For as long as dreams have been reported, there have been stories of both blissful dreams and of terrifying ones—as well as a desire to control the content of dreams. The Native Americans were among the first people to formalize a method of harnessing good dreams and repelling nightmares. Their answer was the "dream catcher." Representations of dream catchers now appear in museums and stores, and some people hang them in their cars as good luck charms. But the history of the dream catcher runs deep, and has serious, spiritual origins.

The dream catcher legend

Dreams hold great significance in Native American tradition. Stories and legends abound of key moments when nightmares heralded disaster. According to Native American beliefs, the night air is filled with the potential for both good and bad dreams—and either can reach the dreamer.

The concept of the dream catcher originated among the Ojibway and Anishnabe tribes. The Ojibway believed that dreams occurred as a result of many factors, but one prominent one was chance—this meant that any individual could be visited by a troubling dream. The wise folk, or "medicine people," sought a means of stopping negative dreams from reaching people. Thus evolved the concept of the dream catcher.

What is a dream catcher?

It is said that an elder of the Anishnabe tribe described a vision that he had had of a spider's web, which was located inside a hoop.

Attached to the web were a feather and a bead. These would hold on to positive dreams, his vision told him, while letting negative dreams pass through. Thus the first dream catchers were made, using willow, the feathers of an owl, and a bead or stone.

Today, the idea of the web continues to play an important part in the meaning and fashioning of dream catchers. Not all dream catchers have stones or beads attached, however.

How it works

The dream catcher is placed above a sleeping area, in a position where it can attract the first rays of the morning light. According to Native American tradition, certain dreams are intended for particular people, conveying messages that are relevant only to them. The dream catcher cannot prevent these dreams from reaching the designated recipient; these dreams will always pass through the web, and the dreamer must dream their important symbols or messages.

The dream catcher can, however, block the free-floating bad dreams that are believed to inhabit the night sky. In the absence of dream catchers, these bad dreams drift unchecked, and can visit sleepers, troubling them. The dream catcher holds back the bad dreams, which are then destroyed by the rays of the early morning sun. It is said that a dream blocked and destroyed in this way cannot revisit the dreamer—nor can it float away to pursue another dreamer.

A good dream is believed to follow the bead or stone into the center of the web, and then into the mind of the person sleeping beneath the dream catcher. The good dreams are allowed to move back and forth through the center of the dream catcher, and can thus be dreamed again, by the same person or by other dreamers.

A feather's breath

It was the grandmothers of the tribe who fashioned the early dream catchers. These were given to newlywed couples, to be placed in their lodges, and also to babies. The dream catcher had a special importance for babies, because of the feather's association with air, and therefore breath, which is crucial to life. The baby would be amused by the swaying of the feather on the dream catcher as it moved through the air, while also learning the importance of pure air and its gift of positive life.

Hoops and webs

In the early part of the 20th century, dream catchers were usually made of a wooden hoop, 3½ inches (87mm) in diameter, which was filled with a web made from nettle-stalk cord. The cord was dyed red with juice from the inner bark of the wild plum, mixed with blood root (to create a deep shade of red).

Dream catchers for babies and children were made from willow and sinew. They were not intended to be long-lasting; as the willow dried, the sinew collapsed—and the dream catcher would fall apart. This disintegration was symbolic of the passing from youth to adulthood.

Today, most dream catchers are made of woven fiber. In certain parts of the northeastern United States and Canada, dream catchers are shaped in the form of a snowshoe or a teardrop.

LUCID DREAMS

Lucid dreams are those in which we are aware that we are dreaming—and in which we have the ability to control the outcome of the dream. Such dreams are rare for most people, but it is possible to teach oneself to dream lucidly. There are, however, mixed opinions about the value of lucid dreaming. Some argue that allowing our consciousness to enter the dream state and exert control over it can be a positive experience, while others consider lucid dreaming to go against the primary function of ordinary dreaming—the expression of the unconscious mind, free from interference.

Conscious dreaming

Reports of what was later termed lucid dreaming have been documented for centuries in many different cultures. In some of the world's main religions, lucid dreaming has mystical associations. In the Hindu and Buddhist traditions, certain people are thought to have the ability to remain conscious while dreaming. Tibetan Buddhists believe that the very purpose of dreaming is to allow the conscious mind to influence and control the unconscious.

The term "lucid dreaming" was coined by a Dutch physician named William Van Eeden in 1913. He reported experiencing mental arousal and a high state of awareness during his dreams.

The moment of realization

Lucid dreams are said to possess a unique quality: once experienced, they are usually remembered. The lucid part of the dream reflects the clarity of the dreamer's level of consciousness rather than the vividness of the dream. The dreamer becomes aware in the middle of such a dream that he or she is dreaming; the dream scenes can become more realistic as this realization occurs. A dreamer who can retain this state of consciousness may then be able to influence the events in the dream.

How to have a lucid dream

Some individuals report having had lucid dreams spontaneously, but for most people, some training is needed. In order to dream lucidly, you must first be able to remember your dreams. As you gain familiarity with dream symbols and with recurrent dream themes, it will become easier to recognize the point in your sleep cycle when dreaming is occurring.

You are more likely to experience a lucid dream when you have had a proper sleep. Relaxation techniques can help you prepare for lucid dreaming. It can also be useful to recite to yourself that when you dream in the night, you will dream lucidly and will be aware that you are experiencing a dream. Keeping a dream diary is another way to induce your mind to engage in lucid dreams. The records in your diary will help you to recognize familiar images and dream scenarios, so that when they recur, you may become consciously aware that your mind has entered the dream state.

In the Buddhist tradition, it is believed that people who are particularly adept in the art of meditation may experience all of their dreams as lucid.

When you sense that you are moving from a period of ordinary to lucid dreaming, it is important to relax. If you can manage not to focus on your conscious mind, but to let yourself "go with the flow," you are likely to be able to continue sleeping and dreaming as you desire. If you can remain in a lucid state, you may be able to reach a new level of consciousness. The more often this happens, the longer the lucidity will last, and the easier it should be to achieve this state on your next attempt.

Deep relaxation and visualization

Meditation, self-hypnosis, and auto-suggestion can all result in a state of consciousness similar to lucid dreaming. These techniques—which also assist in relaxation, and can thus help to bring about a full night's sleep—can help give you a sense of what lucid dreaming is like. They can be self-taught, but are more likely to be successful when learned with the help of a reputable practitioner.

If successful, these techniques will bring about a state of deep relaxation by focusing the mind on breathing; directing it to ignore the continuous interior flow of dialogue, thoughts, and images; and quietly repeating a certain phrase, or mantra. Once you have achieved a state of complete mental and physical calm, you can allow yourself to introduce controlled images into your mind.

These visualizations may consist of a special serene location that you visited in your waking life, or a fantasy place unique to you. Upon reaching this place, spend some imaginary time there relaxing. As with any relaxation technique, visualization does not come magically, and can require persistence to make it work. The more often you practice, however, the easier it will become to achieve this special level of consciousness.

You can also use the achievement of a state of deep relaxation to visualize a difficult situation at work, or in a relationship. Imagine yourself overcoming this challenge—and the outcome of the situation. As with lucid dreaming, this process can help you resolve difficulties in your waking life.

Are lucid dreams dangerous?

No danger or negativity has been reported as resulting from lucid dreaming. In fact, a lucid dream can seem less threatening than an ordinary dream, because you feel that you possess some control over it. If something frightening enters the dream, you can simply make it go away. Similarly, if a work colleague who is causing you problems appears, you can direct yourself to resolve the situation within the dream.

Dream time

Lucid dreams have been used by sleep researchers in an attempt to establish how much time a dream actually occupies. Do dreams condense time, as is widely believed, or do dream events occupy a real time interval? A team of researchers at Stanford University, in California, asked lucid dreamers to carry out previously agreed eye movements to indicate their progression through a predetermined sequence of dream events, and concluded that dream time approximates to real time. Further, they found evidence that dreams may omit unnecessary periods of time that happened in our waking lives, but were not needed in our dreams.

INDEX

CREDITS

Quarto would like to thank and acknowledge the following for their contributions
(key: l left, r right, c centre, t top, b bottom)

P11t *The Dream of Jacob's Ladder*, Frans Francken (1581-1642), The Art Archive
P13b Georgina Martin
P16/17 Clark/Clinch

All other photographs and illustrations are the copyright of Quarto Publishing plc.